Herbert Broom

The Philosophy of Law

being notes of lectures delivered during twenty-three years (1852-1875) in the Inner Temple hall, London

Herbert Broom

The Philosophy of Law
being notes of lectures delivered during twenty-three years (1852-1875) in the Inner Temple hall, London

ISBN/EAN: 9783337238117

Printed in Europe, USA, Canada, Australia, Japan

Cover: Foto ©Thomas Meinert / pixelio.de

More available books at **www.hansebooks.com**

THE PHILOSOPHY OF LAW:

BEING

NOTES OF LECTURES

DELIVERED DURING TWENTY-THREE YEARS

(1852–1875)

IN THE INNER TEMPLE HALL,

LONDON.

BY

HERBERT BROOM, LL.D.,

Late Professor on Common Law to the Inns of Court.

"His utere mecum."—HOR.

NEW YORK:
BAKER, VOORHIS & CO., PUBLISHERS,
66 NASSAU STREET
1876.

Baker & Godwin, Printers,
25 Park Row, N. Y.

PREFACE TO THE AMERICAN EDITION.

The author of the following pages will require no introduction to the legal profession in America. To the general reader it need only be said that Dr. Herbert Broom, as the author of Commentaries on the Common Law, Commentaries on Constitutional Law, and the work on Legal Maxims, has long enjoyed the highest credit and reputation as a writer on legal subjects. As professor on common law to the Inns of Court, London, his lectures for nearly twenty-five years, ending only last year, have been well known to English students; and it is from notes of these lectures that the author has drawn the material, the result of long and careful thought, for a statement of legal principles at once concise, lucid, and comprehensive.

Dr. Broom has only attempted, however, to give, within the compass of this work, the *elements* of the existing law of England. These he has illustrated and enforced by references to the most recent cases and statutes; though, of course, the principles on which they rest were settled centuries ago. Except incidentally, and as needful in the discussion of *principles*, no attempt is made in the following pages to expound rules of evidence and procedure, and merely statutory regulations; but we are given the outlines of that "rational science founded upon the universal principles of moral rectitude," which make the book as instructive and suggestive to the American as to the English reader.

Indeed, the law in its most general sense, regarded as "a rule of conduct," is founded upon principles recognized by all civilized communities; and whatever differences in the mere administration of the law may appear among neighboring states, it will be found that "the reason of the law" is everywhere the same.

But the law, while it concerns itself mainly with principles, is not a fixed science. Its definitions are not fixed and determinate like those of geometry, and are not therefore, and cannot in the nature of things be, certainly and positively expressed. A judge never decides general principles. He decides a case. It is for us to deduce the general principle afterwards. The reason is, that when a legislature promulgates a law, or a judge decides a case, neither of them being superhumanly gifted can foresee cases which must subsequently arise, and which will involve questions of a more complicated and equivocal character, and will then require a new interpretation of the statute, or a modification of the rule of law laid down in the former case.

Courts do not therefore content themselves with merely deciding a particular controversy, and doing justice between the present parties; but they seek to discover and enforce certain principles, just and reasonable in themselves, by which not only the present controversy, but every future controversy of like nature, may be determined.

At the foundation of every legal judgment there is a positive rule of law. To discover this rule by precedent cases—stripping from these cases all that is peculiar to them, not only as to facts, but also as to forms of expression employed by the judges—and by abstraction and induction arrive at the *ratio decidendi*, or that general principle or ground at the foundation of all the decisions on the subject, this is the work of the lawyer and the judge. It is also, in a very high degree, the work of the text writer. It is for him (if he duly magnifies his office and recognizes his high calling) to compare, adjust, and reconcile precedents—to discover their analogies and distinctions—and to give us, as the result, those general rules and principles which lawyers and judges are called upon to apply to the daily concerns of life.

In the following pages Dr. Broom has given his readers only the *results;* he has not given us all the methods by which he has reached them. But aside from its eminently practical character and usefulness to the student and practicing lawyer, the book furnishes a most admirable example of the right method of stating and illustrating legal principles.

New York, July, 1876.

CONTENTS.

CHAPTER I.
PREFATORY OBSERVATIONS.
THE PROVINCE OF LAW.

	PAGE
With what legal science concerns itself	17
Sources of our common law	18
Its doctrines, how enunciated	20
Appellate courts, their functions	22
Legal principles, remarks as to	23
The province of our common law	24
Civil and criminal procedure, how distinguished	25
Tests for distinguishing between them	31

CHAPTER II.
A CONTRACT—WHAT IT IS.

A simple contract, how defined	35
Ingredients in it	36
Privity, what and how exemplified	40
Consent is involved in the idea of contract	43
Ratification, doctrine of, considered	46
An act illegal and void cannot be ratified	48
Implied contract, what, and instances of it	48
The intention of contracting parties, will, if possible be carried out	52

	PAGE
Assessment of damages for breach of contract	56
Liquidated damages, what they are	58
Fraud, how it affects a simple contract	59
Illegality, its effect on a contract	62
Of contracts opposed to public policy	65
The question—what is a contract? briefly answered	66

CHAPTER III.
MERCANTILE CONTRACTS.

A mercantile contract, what it is	68
The ingredients in it considered	69
Privity must exist as between the parties to it	72
The intention of parties may affect their contract	75
add a term to it	79
Mercantile usage may affect a contract	81
by explaining its language	81
by adding a term to it	83
by its inherent authority	85
A mercantile contract may be vitiated by fraud	87
Illegality may affect a mercantile contract	92
Remarks as to mercantile contracts	95

CHAPTER IV.
WRITTEN INSTRUMENTS.

Contracts in writing, how classified	96
Written contracts not required to be in writing	96
Contracts required to be in writing	99
guaranties	101
contracts for the sale of goods	109
Acknowledgments of debts	118
Contracts in writing under seal	119
Characteristics of a deed	120
A bond, what it is, and remarks as to it	123
A covenant, what it is, and remarks as to it	127

CHAPTER V.

LEGAL PRINCIPLES APPLIED TO CONTRACTS.

	PAGE
Introductory observations	133
Instances exemplifying the subject:	
the contract of suretyship	134
check bearing a forged signature	136
policy of life insurance	139
contract performance of which becomes impossible	142
claims against railway companies founded on contract	145
in respect of loss of train	145
personal hurt	147
duties owing by traveller to railway company	151

CHAPTER VI.

A TORT—WHAT IT IS.

Meaning of the word tort	153
Torts to the person, land, or goods	153
Infringements of literary and other rights	156
Rights of action founded on:	
breach of duty	158
negligence	169
malice	187
fraud	192
Tests for determining whether an action for tort is maintainable	194

CHAPTER VII.

LEGAL PRINCIPLES APPLIED TO TORTS.

Introductory observations	197
Instances exemplifying the subject:	
negligence in keeping a bull	198

stealing money deposited with a bank	201
negligence in regard to cattle	202
breach of duty in lending an unruly horse	204
wrongful dealing with jewels pledged	205
bodily hurt done to complainant's servant causing his death	208
right of the finder to bank notes which have been lost	210

CHAPTER VIII.

A CRIME—WHAT IT IS.

Introductory remarks	213
The question—"what is a criminal act?" considered	214
An overt act—what, and how to be proved	215
General characteristics of crime	221
it concerns the public	221
it prejudices the public	221
a guilty intent or mind is an ingredient in it	222
instances of this	223
exceptions to the rule	227
proof of guilty knowledge	227
Criminal acts done forcibly:	
homicide	234
robbery	237
burglary	239
larceny	244
offenses akin to the above	251
Criminal acts involving:	
breach of duty	253
negligence	254
malice	256
fraud	262
Concluding remarks	264

CHAPTER IX.

LEGAL PRINCIPLES APPLIED TO CRIMES.

	PAGE
Introductory observations	267
Instances exemplifying the subject:	
death caused by the kick of a vicious horse .	267
bodily hurt wrongfully caused in pursuit of wild-fowl	268
in the illegal manufacture of fireworks . . .	270
stealing of a lamb	270
things fixed to the freehold . . .	272
wild animals	272
false pretense in selling a gold chain . .	273
fraud on Post Office Savings Bank . .	274
cashier of bank	277
indictment for homicide after conviction for an assault	279
Conclusion	280

*** For References to Cases, &c., cited in the Text, see pp. 281 *et seq.*

Dr. BROOM in his short, modest preface, says this work "exhibits the elements of our existing law, vouched for by reference to recent cases and statutes, though resting on principles which were settled centuries ago;" and submits it "as the result of much thought devoted to the adapting of legal knowledge to the ordinary concerns of life."

THE PHILOSOPHY OF LAW.

CHAPTER I.

PREFATORY OBSERVATIONS.

THE PROVINCE OF LAW.

Jurisprudence is "a rational science, founded upon the universal principles of moral rectitude, but modified by habit and authority."—LORD MANSFIELD.

"Let us consider wherein the law consists, and we shall find it to be, not in particular instances and precedents, but in the reason of the law."—LORD HOLT.

"Il faut des tribunaux." "Ces tribunaux donnent des décisions. Elles doivent être conservées; elles doivent être apprises, pour que l'on y juge aujourd'hui comme l'on y jugea hier, et que la propriété et la vie des citoyens y soient assurées et fixes comme la constitution même de l'état."—MONTESQUIEU.

1. LEGAL science concerns itself with—1st, principles, and 2dly, procedure. The study of procedure, however, is not so attractive as that of principles, nor can the mode of acquiring a knowledge of procedure be made inviting. Principles of law, therefore, not procedure, will in the following pages be expounded; reference being made to rules of evidence, and the mode of proving facts, when needful.

2. Our common law has come to us from very many sources, and having adopted portions of other legal systems, has modified and readjusted them; its province has thus been much extended, and our law has had from time to time not merely to acknowledge new rights, but to devise new remedies. From the Corpus Juris of Justinian—from our Anglo-Saxon ancestors, fragments of whose codes are extant—from customs handed down to us by tradition—from mercantile usages—from the charters of our kings, including some antecedent to the Great Charter—from enactments of the Legislature, and from decided cases, has the common law of England been derived. This vast mass of materials has been drawn and blended together very gradually, and is constantly being added to and altered. Important doctrines of the Roman law especially have been interwoven with our own, and many local customs connected with landed property, of which the origin is lost in antiquity, are still recognized as binding.

3. The province of law is being continually increased by statutory provisions, which either create, alter, or declare, and something is now being done towards the improvement and simplification of our statute book by consolidating, and from time to time codifying, certain branches of the law, and by

expunging from its pages obsolete and repealed enactments. Statutes also—besides creating positive law—have greatly added to, or rendered more definite, the jurisdiction of our courts; very many matters have thus been brought within such jurisdiction, and statutory provisions have sometimes defined the procedure in our courts—have sometimes amplified their powers.

4. Our Legislature usually abstains from interpreting in an authoritative manner a law which it has made; though sometimes it does so by a declaratory enactment. Hence numberless questions as to the construction of statutes have arisen, and the solutions arrived at seem to show that where the language of the Legislature is plain and unambiguous, no considerations of convenience or public policy can influence the court to affix to it a meaning different from its literal and ordinary sense. The court will also strive to give to statutory language its full effect, and will construe one part of a statute by another, so that the whole may, if possible, be operative. Quite recently it was said,[1]* "The acts are the law of the land, and we (the judges) do not sit as a court of appeal from Parliament. We have no authority to act as regents over Parliament, or to refuse to obey a statute

---

* The references to cases will be found at the end of the work.

because of its rigor." Our judges always strive to keep within the spirit, if not within the precise words and literal meaning of an act of Parliament.

5. The doctrines of our law are enunciated in decided cases—now published in an authentic form—and in the treatises of learned writers, of whom Littleton, Coke, and Bacon may especially be named.

Cases which have been judicially recognized and thus have become precedents, must be conformed to, though sometimes, after the lapse of years, they are found to have been erroneously adjudged; when this is so, either the precedents will still be followed, on the ground that it is inexpedient to disturb the established law, or they will be expressly dissented from and overruled.

In a case[2] having reference to the poor law it was observed, *per judicem*: "The case is governed by a long series of decisions. . . . Looking at the reasons for those decisions I think that they are founded on a mistake. Where it is quite clear that there is a mistake, we are not bound to follow a previous case, but we may act here on the maxim, *communis error facit jus*."

6. The above maxim, however, cannot fairly be used for casting opprobrium upon our law. A *dictum*, resolution or judgment which has long been accepted and recognized by the profession will be

dissented from, if shown to have been erroneous; and although the hardship originally caused by it cannot thus be undone, the error at all events will be set right. Of this one notable example must suffice: In a case[3] decided *temp.* Lord Ellenborough (A. D. 1807), it was held that a creditor who had insured the life of his debtor for the amount of his debt, and who after the debtor's death was paid in full by his executors, was precluded from recovering upon the policy. This case was decided wrongly upon a false analogy—the court holding that a policy of life insurance is a contract for indemnity, and that an action upon it is founded on a supposed damnification of the plaintiff occasioned by the death of the assured, existing and continuing to exist at the time of action brought; and reasoning from this analogy the court held that payment of the debt barred the right to recover on the policy. This decision, however, many years after it had been given, was called in question, and the fallacy pervading it was exposed, it being held[4] that a life policy in no way resembles a contract of indemnity; it is a mere contract to pay a sum certain on the death of a person, in consideration of the due payment of a fixed annuity for his life, the amount of the annuity being calculated according to the probable duration of such life. Therefore the plaintiff in the older case ought to have recovered.

7. But although a slip in administering justice sometimes occurs, the authority of decided cases is very great. The reasoning on which a judgment rests is almost invariably given, and Lord Mansfield, we are told,[5] endeavored "to render the tribunal where he presided not only the instrument of immediate justice, but an instructive seminary to such as were engaged in professional studies."

In the appellate tribunals judicial errors are for the most part set right, and uniformity in the exposition of law is thus to a great extent insured. Were no right of appeal allowed to an unsuccessful suitor, "it would be very easy for judges by construction and interpretation to change even a written law, and it would be most easy for the judges of the common laws of England, which are not written, but depend upon usage, to make a change in them."[6]

The judges of our appellate courts must get legal knowledge from the same sources as inferior judges, but their duty sometimes is to examine precedents *de novo*, and in doing so they may find that a long course of precedents has originated in mistake, or that the opinion of the profession upon a particular point has been erroneous. Admitting the difference between a decision or a precedent in a Court whence appeal lies and in a court of the last resort, the highest court is bound to view with respect the practice, decisions and precedents in the court below as evidence of the law, and only to overrule a decision in which the law has been mistaken. The main difference between the supreme and the inferior court is this: the latter might feel itself bound by its own precedents, though erroneous, whereas by the former such precedents would be overruled.[7]

8. Leading principles regulate and govern every department of our law, though they are sometimes applied with modifications in order that justice may be done. Nor need any such modification of a legal principle, when it occurs, surprise us, because the relations of individuals to each other in this country, and the rights or liabilities which result from their dealings together, are exceedingly diversified, founded in part on the feudal law, in part on our customary unwritten law, and in part founded on our law merchant, which is of comparatively recent extraction, and yet may challenge in importance comparison with the other two.

9. An apparent conflict between legal principles may often be explained on close examination of the facts to which they were respectively applied. And throughout this volume every proposition laid

down has either been illustrated by facts upon which judgment has actually been pronounced, or has been vouched by reference to the point and *ratio decidendi* of a case, or the principles deducible therefrom. These matters have been carefully considered, so that the reader, if unwilling or unable consult the report itself, may feel reasonable confidence that the extract from it set before him is correct.

10. The province of our common law, *i. e.*, of our law as administered in the common law divisions of the High Court of Justice and on appeal from judgments there given, as well as in the county courts, and some other inferior tribunals, may be thus shortly stated.

Our common law concerns itself, 1st, with contentious matters arising between private persons; 2dly, with matters affecting the community. It supplies remedies, therefore, for infringement of private rights, and inflicts punishment for offenses against the public. Many other and dissimilar matters, to which specific reference cannot be made in this work, also come under the cognizance of our courts; *ex. gr.*, questions connected with the administration of the poor law—with sanitary enactments—statutes regulating municipal corporations, railway companies and associations, incorporated or otherwise—are daily argued before them and resolved. Such matters, I repeat, how important soever they may be to the welfare of society or of individuals, cannot here be taken notice of. They stand somewhat apart from the ordinary routine and *curriculum* of law, and have been separately treated of by writers of established name and reputation.

11. Suffice it here to say that civil procedure is for the most part made ancillary to the asserting of private rights, whilst criminal procedure is principally directed towards insuring these objects—the maintenance of the public peace, the observance of morality, at all events where any deflection from it might tend to prejudice the public; criminal procedure is designed also for insuring the stability of the property, the security of the person of every member of the community.

The considerations necessary for determining whether a private right has been violated are different from those appropriate for deciding whether punishment should ensue upon an act.

12. Thus an action for a trespass to land is founded on the idea that complainant's right to the exclusive occupancy and enjoyment of it has been wrongfully interfered with. He alleges, for instance, his ownership and occupancy of a certain

farm, through a part of which runs a private road, bounded by a hedge, and separated from plaintiff's fields on either side; that defendant had wrongfully claimed to use this road for his horses and carriages as being a public road, though warned that it was not such; that on a day specified defendant came with a cart and horse, servants and workmen, forcibly used the road, and broke down and removed a gate placed across it by the plaintiff; further, that defendant then with his servants and workmen damaged plaintiff's hedge, and so forth.

The wrong here complained of is clearly a private wrong, with which, if involving no riot or breach of the peace, the public is not concerned. If, however, a public road or footway be obstructed by a gate placed across it, a public nuisance would be created, in respect of which an indictment might be maintained; for our criminal law tries to protect rights by prohibiting undue interference with them, and by annexing punishment to an infraction of them. The rights of property it scrupulously guards, discriminating, however, between rights the infringement of which may be alarming or dangerous to the public, and rights of which the invasion may, as between man and man, be reasonably compensated by pecuniary damages.

13. The nature of a private duty, *i. e.*, of a duty owing by one man to another, may be illustrated by the case of an excavation unjustifiably made so near to the confines of a neighbor's land, that his house, which has acquired a prescriptive right to support, in consequence thereof sinks and becomes ruinous. Here the duty violated is obviously not owing to the public at large, but to one individual in particular—the owner of the adjoining land and house. The breach of such a duty under the conditions stated is actionable,[8] not indictable.

A question not long since arose—whether a duty was imposed on a dock company to provide access to and egress from a ship in a dock, and as to their liability for damage caused by their allowing a dangerous gangway to be used. It was held that a duty was imposed upon the dock company either to have made the gangway safe, or to have given notice of its dangerous condition to the plaintiff, who had gone on board a ship on business.[9]

Questions as to the existence, nature and obligatory force of duties alleged to be owing by one man to another, are continually arising, and many such will be stated and discussed in Chapters VI and VII of this volume.

14. Fraud may be directed against an individual

specifically or against the public. Let us suppose that the vendor of a jewel is guilty of deceit in selling it—that he is shown to have been actually and fraudulently cognizant of the falsehood of some representation made by him with respect to it—that he has sold it as and for that which it is not; under such circumstances the vendor will be liable to a civil action for the fraud of which he has been guilty, and the damage thence resulting.[10]

The essence of the misdemeanor of cheating at common law is a design to impose on the credulity of others, and to induce them to believe a thing that is not true—this being usually done to benefit the defendant, and always "to the evil example" of the community. These last words indicate the distinction between a public and a private fraud—between the species of fraud which ought to be repressed and punished, and that kind of fraud aimed at an individual rather than at the public, against which a man should be upon his guard, and which, if committed to his detriment, is actionable only.

15. Cases involving fraud are often under the notice of our courts, and the line is extremely fine which separates indictable from merely actionable fraud. Where goods sent on approval are, whilst unpaid for, wrongfully converted by their recipient

to his own use—or again, where goods are sold or pledged, and money is thus obtained in respect of them by some false statement as to their quality—the nicest questions may arise. In the one case, were the goods converted with an intention to steal them? In the other case, was there fraud affecting the public, or was it so entirely mixed up with contract as to come within the definition of a private fraud? Do the proofs adduced point rather to undue exaggeration of the quality and goodness of a chattel than to misrepresentation?[11]

A fraud mixed up with contract lies indeed upon the very confines which separate the civil and the criminal law. A man may make himself liable to an action, because he has stated something which went beyond the exact line of truth, or has concealed some material fact which ought to have been made known to the other contracting party. A man may honestly misrepresent—he may state as true something which he believes to be true, but which turns out to be untrue. Whereas to support a criminal charge, proof of the *scienter*, or guilty knowledge, must be given, and of an intention to deceive and defraud in doing what is charged against the defendant. Hence is the impossibility in some cases of affixing criminal liability to the promoters or the directors of a company, who, by circulating false statements respecting its affairs, have induced third persons to become shareholders in it to their great detriment.[12]

16. A conspiracy is an agreement to effect an unlawful purpose, or to effect a lawful purpose by unlawful means, and such an agreement is by the common law of England an indictable offense. It is, indeed, fit that, if several persons deliberately plot mischief to an individual or to the State, they should be liable to punishment, although they may have done no act in execution of their scheme. For, where several persons thus concert together, confederate and combine, our law apprehends danger to the community from the mere fact of such confederacy; persons so acting are, therefore, indictable, even though the object aimed at may never be accomplished, or may, if accomplished, in itself be unobjectionable. If, however, there be the fact of combination or confederacy and evidence of intent, these proofs will not necessarily suffice for conviction upon a charge of conspiracy. For instance, an agreement amongst themselves by members of Parliament to make defamatory speeches in the House of Commons respecting an individual not being a member of the house would not be indictable.[13] More harm would accrue to the public from restricting the freedom of debate in Parlia-

ment than from the agreement and confederacy supposed.

17. What tests then should be applied to an act for determining whether it be criminal or not? They will be indicated in Chapter VIII of this volume. The primary tests, however, have been already stated. Does the act in question prejudice or tend to prejudice the public? Was it directed against the community at large rather than against an individual? Is it punishable?

The character of criminalty may be impressed on an act either by the common or by the statute law. An act of violence to the person is *prima facie* criminal as of evil example, against the peace, causing alarm to the public and a sense of want of security. So a nuisance prejudicial to the public is indictable, whereas in order that an action may be maintainable by a private person for that which amounts to a public nuisance, three things must be established: 1st. Plaintiff must show some particular damage to himself beyond that which is suffered by the rest of the public; 2dly. The damage must be shown to have been direct; 3dly. It must be shown to have been substantial, not fleeting or evanescent.[14]

18. A customer gives to a carrier goods of a dangerous description to carry—requiring, there-

fore, more caution in their conveyance than ordinary merchandise—a duty becomes thus imposed by law upon the customer of this kind to give notice of the dangerous character of his goods to the carrier, in order that they may be carried with that degree of care, the absence whereof might entail danger on the carrier or his servants. The breach of this duty, if productive of damage, will be actionable. Suppose that a person puts on board ship goods which are of a combustible and inflammable nature, the owner would clearly be liable to any one injured in consequence of their combustion, by reason of his wrongful omission to give notice of the nature of the goods which he put on board.[15] In such a case the duty violated is declared by the common law, and although in general the obligations owing from a customer to the carrier, or *vice versa*, fall within the class of private rather than of public duties, it is conceivable that the breach of such a duty, as stated, might seriously concern the public, and so be criminally punishable. Indeed, the Court of King's Bench, many years since, considered the precise state of facts last put, and said that if a customer knowingly send on board ship goods of a dangerous kind without giving notice thereof—considering the peril so caused to the lives of those on board—the act amounts to a species of delinquency for which the actor will be criminally liable and punishable.[16]

19. Our law, as between party and party, tries to protect rights, usually by awarding pecuniary damages for wrongful interference with them; sometimes by compelling the restoration of property or the performance of this or that thing by the party in default, and sometimes in other ways. Occasionally an aggrieved person is allowed to redress his grievance for himself.

Subject to the condition that no riot be committed, a nuisance may sometimes be abated, *i. e.*, removed and put a stop to, by the person whom it injuriously affects.[17] The treasurer of a county court has been held justified in breaking open the offices of the registrar of the court, during the absence of that official, in order to get at the books kept by him, with a view to their being audited.[18] Here no breach of the peace could have ensued from the act of violence in question. So if A. take goods out of the actual possession of B. against his will, B. may justify using force for retaking the goods, and so may set up a good ground of defense in an action of assault; and if goods are obtained under color of a contract of sale, but really by trick and fraud, the semblance of a contract disappears—

the property in the goods does not pass, and they may be recaptured.[19]

The law allows the commission of an assault in such a case, because the remedy by action would be dilatory, tedious, and perhaps inadequate.

20. An individual then, it must be admitted, is sometimes allowed to take the law into his own hands, and "right himself." The general rule, however, proved or tested by the exceptions to it, has prescribed the procedure by action or by indictment as applicable respectively for the redress of a private grievance, no matter what its precise nature, and for the vindication of public justice. Therefore, throughout this book, the references have almost exclusively been made to cases thus raising—by action or on indictment—legal questions, curious, interesting or important. In dealing with facts out of which any such question is evolved, everything superfluous or irrelevant must be put aside, so that the very gist and essence of the matter may be got at.

CHAPTER II.

A CONTRACT—WHAT IT IS.

"Un contrat est une espèce de convention . . une convention . . est le consentement de deux ou de plusieurs personnes, pour former entre elles quelque engagement, ou pour en résoudre un précedent, ou pour le modifier."—POTHIER.

21. LAW being a science, the use of technical words in discussing it can scarcely be avoided; the following explanatory definitions of certain terms used in this chapter are therefore at once put before the reader. The word "contract" conveys the idea of persons being drawn together in respect of some subject-matter and by some common motive; a "simple contract," of which alone I shall here speak, is evidenced and authenticated by writing not under seal (*post*, Chapter IV), by words, conduct, and so forth; "privity" indicates the tie between and connecting parties. The word "contract" includes the idea of "privity." It involves also the idea of "consent"—that the parties have agreed to do or not to do something, which ought to be defined. Consent, moreover, may assume the form of "ratification"—of assent subsequent.

22. Although a "contract" is equivalent to an "agreement," it is in legal contemplation composite, involving three ingredients, viz., a request, a consideration or *quid pro quo*, and a promise: a request from the contractor to the contractee to do or to refrain from doing a specified thing; a doing of or refraining from the thing specified, or at all events an undertaking or engagement to such effect by the contractee; and a promise thereupon by the contractor to benefit by payment of money or otherwise the contractee. And in every simple contract, written, verbal, or partly evidenced by writing, partly by word of mouth or the conduct of the parties, for breach of which an action will lie, there must have been either express or implied the ingredients mentioned, viz., the request, the consideration, and the promise.

23. Familiarity with the above-mentioned ingredients in a simple contract may be needed for testing its validity, inasmuch as one or other of them may disappear on applying to it the touchstone of a legal principle. For instance, a father could not be held liable even for necessary food and clothing supplied by the plaintiff, a tradesman, for the use of his infant son, unless there were evidence to show either that the goods in question were ordered to be supplied by the father, or that

their user and enjoyment by the son received the father's sanction.[20] The father would otherwise have been an entire stranger to the transaction— there would have been no request nor consent by him, nor privity as between him and the tradesman who supplied the goods.

24. Addressing myself for the moment to legal students, I would insist on the importance of testing one's aptitude in singling out and distinguishing between one and another of these main ingredients in a simple contract. The ingredients enumerated seem familiar enough, the order in which they have been mentioned seems natural and proper, yet it may not always be found easy to indicate with certainty and precision where in a contract obviously enforceable at law—for breach of which an action would lie—each of these ingredients is to be detected, how it is to be evidenced and established. Nor must this sort of self-examination be declined as too elementary or as unnecessary, for sometimes, in relation to some essential ingredient in a simple contract, differences of opinion have existed on the bench, and sometimes the ingredient is not easily to be discerned.[21]

25. As in the next chapter the consideration for a promise will have to be specially exemplified, I can here give but one or two instances of it. A.

being indebted to B., dies, and then B. assigns the debt to C., and empowers him to receive it. Moreover, D., who is A.'s executor, promises to pay it him. Will an action lie at suit of C. against D. to compel payment of the debt? Assuming that the statutory requirements as to written evidence of the agreement have been complied with, and that a memorandum of the contract signed by D., the party sought to be charged on it, is forthcoming (*post*, Chap. IV), there would still be an insurmountable obstacle to C.'s success in such an action. Our law insists that there shall be a consideration for a promise to pay money. It thus protects persons who are too free-handed, are reckless and improvident. The breach of a *nudum pactum* will not sustain an action.[22] If in the case put D. had promised to pay in consideration of C.'s forbearance to press and sue for the debt, an action might have lain at suit of the latter party against the former for the sum claimed; moreover the compromise of a disputed claim made *bona fide* may be the consideration for a promise, even though it ultimately appears that the claim was wholly unfounded and unenforceable. "Every day a compromise is effected on the ground that the party making it has a fair chance of succeeding, and if he *bona fide* believes he has a fair chance of success, he has a reasonable ground for suing, and his forbearance to sue will constitute a good consideration." [23]

26. An action may be maintainable upon the express ground that there was a want of consideration in some prior dealing between the parties to it, or that the consideration supposed to have existed has failed altogether or in part. Thus an action may lie to recover money paid under a mistake of fact. No man should be deprived of money which he has thus parted with, and where it is against justice and conscience that the receiver should retain it. If A. pays money to B., supposing him to be the agent of C., to whom he owes the money, and B. is not such agent, it may be recovered back. If A. and B. are settling an account and make a mistake in summing up the items, and A. pays B. 100*l*. too much, A. may recover it back. In any such case, not only was the money paid under a mistake by the party paying it, but the retention of the money by its recipient would be against equity and good faith.[24]

It not unfrequently happens also that where a transaction has taken place between parties, a state of things arises in reference to it which was not contemplated by them, but is such that one party ought in justice and fair dealing to pay a sum of money to the other; and then, to support an action for it, the consideration being apparent in the money which has got into defendant's pocket, the request that it may and promise that it shall be repaid, if not express, will be implied in law.

27. Our common law, however, sometimes declines to imply a promise to pay money which might seem to have been fairly earned; as on the part of the client or the patient to remunerate his counsel or physician for work professionally done at his request. The general rule is that any man who bestows his labor for another has a right of action to recover from him compensation for that labor. But the law supposes a physician or a barrister to act without pecuniary remuneration, and declines to imply any promise which would be counter to such presumption. This rule or rather presumption of our common law is founded on public policy, and in the case of the barrister—though not in that of the physician—is so stringent that it countervails even an express contract for remuneration. A special contract cannot have efficacy where there is thus an incapacity to contract.[25]

28. The word "contract," properly understood, involves the idea of "privity" and of "consent" (Art. 21); if there be no privity between parties, there can be no contract or agreement between them. Why should a man be bound by stipula-

tions to which he is altogether a stranger—to which he has not expressly or impliedly assented?

In a recent case the facts were of this kind: Plaintiff, an officer in command of troops conveyed over the Great Indian Peninsular Railway, sued that company for loss of luggage caused by defendants' alleged negligence. To this action a defense was successfully set up, that when the loss occurred the plaintiff with his luggage was being conveyed under a contract between the defendants and the Indian Government, and that there was no contract with the plaintiff.[26] The ground of decision in this case is widely applicable.

Let us further suppose such a state of things as this. A. contracts with B. and undertakes to lay down a gas-pipe for him fit and proper for supplying gas from the main—the construction of the piping is defective, and gas escapes, whereupon C., a third person, unconnected with A., by negligently using a light to ascertain the cause of the escape explodes the gas, and so produces damage. Upon these facts A. will be liable to B. for breach of contract in not having laid down a proper pipe; he will not be relieved from liability by reason that the immediate cause of the explosion was the act of C. C. will be responsible to B. for his negligent and wrongful conduct, in accordance with principles hereafter stated (Chap. VI). As between A. and B., there is privity in virtue of their contract. As between A. and C., there is no privity.[27]

29. An apparent lack of privity between parties may sometimes be supplied by the usage of a particular trade or profession: for instance, where personal property is settled before marriage the practice is that the lady's solicitor should draw the settlement, and that the intended husband should have the privilege of paying for it.[28]

30. With the rule requiring privity in a contract has long existed contemporaneously another well-known rule, which forbids the assignment of a mere right or *chose in action;* the assignee of such a right cannot sue the original contractor, for as between these parties there is no privity. Where a right to sue in contract has become vested in A., enforceable against C., A. cannot assign or hand over to B. the same right, to be enforced against the same person in the name of B., though A. might for due consideration or by deed bind himself to sue C. for the benefit of B. To this rule exceptions have been allowed in deference to mercantile usage, or have been created by statute. Bills of exchange, promissory notes, checks, policies of life and marine insurance,[29] and certain other securities, are assignable. To some instruments, which are assignable

under the law merchant, brief reference will hereafter be made.

The doctrine which forbade the assignment of a chose in action, though somewhat relaxed, was in ancient times very necessary; its observance tended to repress litigation, to prevent the wealthy and litigious from buying up rights of action to the detriment of their poorer neighbors; and the enforcement of this rule, subject to relaxations in favor of trade, was, doubtless, beneficial in repressing fraud and simplifying the mode of proof. Under the judicature acts the rule in question has been modified only, not abrogated.

31. The reader having already inferred that "contract" involves the idea of "consent," as to this point little more need here be said. Upon a dispute between the overseers of two parishes respecting the election of a sexton, and the payment of his salary, one of the parishes paid the sexton without the consent of the other, and brought an action for the money as paid for their use, whereupon Lord Mansfield said: "The dispute arises concerning the election of a sexton, and the way of trying it is by refusing to pay the sexton elected: the whole is notoriously in litigation. Under these circumstances, therefore, one parish paid the quota of the other in spite of their teeth. Then can it be

said that this action for money paid, laid out and expended, will lie? Certainly not. This action must be grounded either on an express or an implied consent: here is neither."[30]

From a proposition so simple as that "a contract implies consent," deductions useful in the daily routine of life may readily be drawn. Thus, where A. relies upon a contract in writing, consisting of an offer to and acceptance by B., he should consider whether there be, on the proofs adducible, evidence of a complete contract or agreement binding upon B. "If one man offers to let a house or to sell goods to another upon certain terms, and the other writes back, 'I agree to take the house or to purchase the goods upon those terms,' that amounts to a complete agreement." But if the reasonable construction of the alleged offer and acceptance shows that something material as between the contracting parties is left to be afterwards arranged—that the mind of the defendant never assented to all the terms proposed, never was at one with the mind of the plaintiff—there would be no sufficient acceptance of the offer made to bind the defendant—there would be no agreement between him and plaintiff for breach of which an action would be maintainable.[31]

There must be a complete mutual assent to the

terms of a simple contract, in order that it may be valid and reciprocally binding. This consent it is which justifies the law of every civilized country in holding a contractor to his contract.

32. Since a contract is founded in consent, it follows that where there is an incapacity to consent, there is an incapacity to contract. Wherefore a contract executed under duress may be avoided, and the contract of an infant, a married woman, or a lunatic, is in general voidable or void.

A married woman is, for various reasons, favorably regarded by the common—unwritten—law. She is deemed to be under the power and coercion of her husband; she has no property save such as may have been settled to her separate use, and is consequently incapacitated from making good any claims against her; and besides this, her separate existence is held to have become merged in that of her husband, so that, except in certain cases, she can at common law only contract as agent for him, not in her own right and as a principal.[32] Innovation has been made upon this doctrine of our law by a recent statute.[33]

An infant, under the age of twenty-one years, is also specially protected in respect of contracts which might be prejudicial to him, as well by our customary as by our written law.[34]

33. Ratification is the act of giving sanction and validity to something done by another person. It is an adoption of a contract previously made in the name of the ratifying party.

A contract when capable of being ratified must have been good in itself; if simple it must have been made upon consideration. If it were not so, the adoption or ratification of it would be of no avail. What a ratification is meant to cure is the want of authority in the party who made the contract in the name of another. A *prima facie* contract, which was void when made, could not be ratified.

34. Thus, the promoters of a joint stock company could not sue the company when formed for preliminary expenses, on the ground of an entire want of privity as between the projectors and the company, nor could the company, if so disposed, ratify any contract for payment of those expenses, such contract having been made when the company was non-existent.[35] In such a case as this there is neither previous assent nor privity in law, nor is there efficient ratification.

Recently the following facts appeared in evidence: A proposal made by plaintiff to A., B., and C. (defendants), "on behalf of" a projected hotel company, to sell certain goods at a price specified—

acceptance of such proposal in writing by defendants signing "on behalf of" the company—subsequent incorporation of the company under the joint stock companies' act, 1862—and an attempted ratification of the antecedent written contract. Upon these facts would A., B., and C. be liable upon the contract? or would the company be liable in virtue of their so-called ratification of it? These queries must be thus answered. At the time when A., B., and C. contracted, there was no principal besides themselves in existence, and ratification can only be by an existing person, on whose behalf the contract might have been made at the time.[86] Under the circumstances put, if the plaintiff had consented to accept the company, when constituted, as purchasers of his goods, and as his debtors, in lieu of A., B., and C., a new contract might thus have been created, but such an arrangement would not have been tantamount to ratification.

So, if contracts have been entered into by the directors of a company, which were beyond the scope and limits of the objects of the company as set forth in their memorandum of association, and were consequently not merely voidable but absolutely void under the provisions of the joint stock companies' act, 1862, already cited; the contracts having been thus *extra vires*, and still-born originally, it would be beyond the power of the shareholders to give life to them by any subsequent attempted ratification.[87]

Cases such as cited in the three preceding paragraphs throw strong light on the doctrine of ratification, and have much practical importance.

35. An act illegal and void cannot be ratified. In a case not long since adjudged the facts were these: The defendant's name was forged to a joint and several promissory note, and whilst the note was current the defendant, protesting that the signature was not his, in order to prevent the prosecution of the forger, put his name to a memorandum setting forth that he held himself responsible for the note. It was adjudged that this memorandum could not be construed as a ratification, inasmuch as the act which it professed to ratify was illegal and void, and incapable of being ratified. If the meaning of the memorandum was that the defendant agreed to be responsible on the note in consideration that plaintiff would forbear to prosecute the forger, such an agreement was altogether void as against the policy of the law.[88]

36. Parties may doubtless so contract, whether by writing, by word of mouth, or otherwise, that nothing is left to implication or intendment of law, the parties having determined their respective

rights and obligations for themselves. Often, however, they will be found not to have sufficiently provided for possible contingencies; if so, legal principles may need to be called into operation, to complete as it were by implication the provisions of the contract, and to adjust the rights and obligations of the parties to it. When such a state of things has occurred, and this has been accomplished, the final result will be what it would have been if an express contract containing the terms implied, together with those of the original agreement, had been entered into. For instance, an engineer agrees to do certain work to be paid for by quarterly installments ranging over a certain time; he dies after so many installments have become due, but before completion of the work. Should the law hold that the personal representatives of the deceased are entitled to the instalments due at the time of death, the result would be the same as if the contingency of death had been foreseen and provided for in the contract, and had not been left to be provided for by the law.[39]

A., we will suppose, engages B.'s wife to perform and sing at a concert, nothing being said as to any possible cause of absence through physical incapacity for doing so; such a cause of incapacity arises, whereby A., being unable to obtain a substitute, sustains pecuniary loss; what is the law applicable on view of these facts for determining A.'s right of action and B.'s liability? The judge at the trial of the cause would direct the jury that there was in law an implied condition annexed to the contract, that the illness of the wife should discharge the husband from performance of it, and the verdict, on proof of the facts supposed, would be returned accordingly.[40]

37. Any case such as just cited throws light on the meaning of the term "implied" contract, and shows that the liability of either party to a contract will be the same whether from given facts or data a contract be implied by law and inferred by a jury, or whether an express contract identical therewith be actually proved and put in evidence; the facts and data being on the one supposition deposed to at Nisi Prius, the express contract being on the other supposition proved—if wholly written, by producing it—if partly written and partly verbal, by writing, by witnesses, and so forth.

Another instance of a condition being imported into a contract is offered by a contract for personal service. Such a contract having been made, containing no stipulation to the contrary, should the servant die, his representatives could not be compelled to perform the service in his stead, or pay damages, and equally by the death of the master, the servant is discharged.⁴¹ Here, on the happening of a contingency, the law is called upon to supply a term in the particular contract, and to say what should be done as between the contracting parties.

38. By reference to the theory of implied contracts and undertakings, a case may often be at once decided as between litigating parties. Thus, should a solicitor commit a breach of the implied duty imposed on him by his retainer, the moment such breach of duty is committed, a cause of action accrues against him.⁴² A solicitor employed to sue for a debt in the county court, has no implied authority, after obtaining judgment, to enter into an agreement with the debtor not to enforce such judgment for a stipulated time; and should the judgment be enforced by execution before that time has expired, the principal so enforcing it, will not be liable unless he has authorized or assented to the act of his solicitor.⁴³ The non-liability of the principal is a logical deduction from the absence of implied authority in the agent.

39. To put a case quite dissimilar from the preceding. If a horse is sold with a warranty of soundness, and it turns out to be unsound, the purchaser cannot return the horse, unless there is

a stipulation in the agreement empowering him to do so if the horse should not answer to the warranty; all that the purchaser can do in the absence of such stipulation is to offer to return the horse to the seller, and if the seller refuses to receive back the horse, then the purchaser may sell the horse and recover the difference in price from the vendor."[44] Here the contracting parties are to blame, if they do not expressly provide beforehand for the happening of the particular contingency. When, as very often befalls, parties are not thus circumspect, our law applies to the state of facts before it rules which, in the abstract, have long since been settled.

Where goods have been sold by sample, and the purchaser "desires to rescind his purchase, upon the ground that the quality of the goods does not correspond with the sample, it is his duty to make a distinct offer to return, or in fact to return the goods, by stating to the vendor that the goods are at his risk—that they do not belong to the purchaser—that the purchaser rejects them—that he throws them back upon the vendor's hands—and that the contract is rescinded." [45]

40. It will not, of course, be supposed from anything which has thus far been said, that our law disregards the declared or presumable intention of

contracting parties; a contrary inference would be correct. Our law exercises much ingenuity in trying to ascertain what the parties meant, and in striving to carry out and make operative their intentions; of this a very few instances must suffice.

At common law, materials worked by one into the property of another become part thereof, whether such property be fixed or movable. Bricks built into a wall become part of the house —thread stitched into a coat which is under repair, or planks and nails worked into a ship under repair, become part of the coat or of the ship—and therefore generally, and in the absence of something to show a contrary intention, the bricklayer, tailor, or shipwright is to be paid for the work and materials done and provided, although the whole work be not complete. Such is, *primâ facie, i. e.*, at common law, the nature of the contract for doing work and supplying materials. The essence of such contract may, however, be altered and differently modeled by the expressed intentions of the parties to it. The workman may agree to complete the entire work, and to receive payment when the whole is complete, and not before. If such be the agreement, the plaintiff, having contracted to do an entire work for a specific sum, can recover nothing unless the work be done, or unless it can be shown that it was the defendant's fault that the work was incomplete, or unless there is something to justify the conclusion that the parties entered into a fresh contract.[46]

41. Let us suppose that a check bears on the back of it the name and signature of a former holder—what, it may be asked, is the precise significance thereto attaching? Does it fix him with any, and, if so, with what sort of liability? Or is he unaffected thereby, *i. e.*, is he in the same position as any other holder *pro tempore* of the instrument, and not liable to be sued upon it? The question proposed must be answered on reference to the intention with which the signature was placed upon the check. A check payable to bearer may doubtless be indorsed in the full and complete sense of that word. It is, however, of common occurrence that a name is signed on the back of such an instrument meant as an acknowledgment of or receipt for the amount for which it was drawn, or as indicating that the check is paid in to the credit of a particular account; at all events, not intended in any way to operate as an indorsement; and when a man's name is written on the back of such an instrument without the intention of indorsing and making himself liable upon it, our law holds that he is not so liable. Here, as in many

other cases, it considers the intent accompanying the act under notice, with a view to determining its character, and declines to saddle with responsibility as indorser, one who had no intention of incurring it.[47]

42. With a view to carrying out the intention of parties, it has been held that there may be an actionable breach of a contract before the time for complete performance of it has arrived.[48] An action for breach of promise to marry the plaintiff after the death of the defendant's father may be maintainable before the death has happened, *ex. gr.*, should the defendant in the mean time declare his intention never to fulfill his promise, and so repudiate and rescind it.[49]

43. Persons are generally free to contract as they please, conforming to the requirements of the customary or statute law, and if a contract, in no respect infringing legal principles, be entered into, and be suffered to remain unrescinded, a jury—proof being giving of the breach of contract—will be directed that nominal damages at all events are recoverable, although no actual or substantial damage may have accrued from the breach; the reason being that the law holds every man to his contract. If then a man positively undertakes for the happening of a particular event, he may, if it should not

happen, incur liability for damages; nor is there any hardship in this, because the possibility of the event not happening must be supposed to have been in his contemplation when he made the contract.⁵⁰ To this rule, which is obviously founded in common sense, reference will again be made, and some qualifications of it will hereafter be specified. (Chaps. III, and IV.)

44. As regards the assessment of damages for breach of contract, it may here be opportune to observe that the party contracting or undertaking —and thus assuming an obligation which he is bound at the risk of paying damages to perform —can at most be made liable for such damages only as might naturally have flowed from the breach of contract, or as might reasonably have been brought within his contemplation by notice or otherwise when he entered into the contract or assumed the obligation. A notice might indeed be so given as to be incorporated with and form part of the contract.

Primâ facie, damage actually resulting from a breach of contract is recoverable, provided it be such as may fairly be considered as arising directly, *i. e.,* in the ordinary course of things, from such breach. If a man contracts to carry a chattel, and loses it, he must pay its value, though he may discover that the chattel was more valuable than he had supposed. When, however, the loss is not such as would in the ordinary course of things naturally arise from the breach of contract, but is of an exceptional nature, in the absence of some notice to the defendant of special circumstances, damages cannot be given for the loss.

45. What has been stated in the preceding article may be thus exemplified. A., being a goods carrier, takes for conveyance machinery to be put up in a mill, without which the mill cannot work; he has no notice of the purpose for which the machinery is intended; if the machinery be lost *in transitu*, the carrier could not be made responsible for pecuniary damages in respect of the stoppage of the mill.[51]

Recently a court of law was called on to discriminate between two items of damages claimed— one for inconvenience caused through breach of duty by a railway company in conveying H. and his wife to a wrong terminus, and another for illness caused by their having to walk home from such terminus in inclement weather, and consequent medical expenses. The former of these heads of damage was allowed as the immediate result of breach of duty by defendants. The latter head of damage claimed was disallowed, as being merely connected with the breach of duty by "a series of causes" intervening between the immediate consequence of the breach of duty and the damage complained of.[52]

Again, the plaintiff, a commercial traveler, had sent his case of goods by luggage train from Oxford to Liverpool without making any intimation respecting it of any kind. There was a delay of two days *in transitu*. The plaintiff, however, was held not entitled to recover the hotel expenses incurred by him whilst awaiting the arrival of the package. In any such case the question for the jury will be—has there been undue delay? If so, nominal damages, at all events, should be given, but it is difficult to see how the hotel expenses could be considered as naturally resulting from non-delivery of the parcel, or how they could be said to have been reasonably in the contemplation of the parties when they made the contract.[58]

46. The assessment of damages for breach of contract may be affected and facilitated by stipulations of the parties having reference to the contingency of a breach occurring, and specifying an amount to be paid in that event as and for liquidated, ascertained, and predetermined damages by the one party to the other. If, indeed, from the terms used such sum is to be paid rather as a pen-

alty for non-performance of the contract than as liquidated damages, a court of law, adopting an equitable principle, allows the jury to assess the damages at less than the named amount, which is thus treated as the limit—not as the precise measure—of the damages. Upon this particular point nice distinctions are often taken in interpreting a contract.[54]

47. Where A. is brought into contact with B. in a matter purely of contract, a duty is imposed upon A. of this kind—to conduct himself honestly towards B., not necessarily disclosing everything in prejudice of the subject-matter of the contract, but answering questions concerning it truthfully, and by no means volunteering statements inducing to the contract, false or which are based in fraud. *Crescit in orbe dolus*—and fraud, we are told,[55] is where one man endeavors to gain a personal advantage to himself, either by concealment of the truth or by inducing another to believe that to be true which is not so. If, moreover, persons take upon themselves to make false assertions as to which they are ignorant whether such assertions are true or untrue, they must in a civil point of view be held as responsible as if they had asserted that which they knew to be untrue.[56]

48. The effect of fraud upon a contract is of this

kind,—it renders the contract voidable by or at the election of the person upon whom such fraud has been practiced. It gives him an option to rescind the contract.[57]

That which bears the semblance of a contract may thus be vitiated by fraud, and the apparent right founded upon the contract may thus be put aside. So long since as Lord Coke's time it was held that if an illiterate person have a deed falsely read over to him, and he then seals and delivers the parchment, that parchment is nevertheless not his deed.[58] A like principle may be applied to a contract not under seal. If a man write his name across the back of a blank bill stamp, and part with it, and the paper is afterwards improperly filled up, he is nevertheless liable as indorser, because he intended—when signing his name—to indorse a bill of exchange to be afterwards filled up, leaving the amount, the date, the maturity, and the principal parties to the bill undetermined. Here was no fraud inducing to the contract and so vitiating it. Now let us suppose that the party was led to indorse the bill upon the assurance that it was some other instrument, for instance a guaranty (Chap. IV)—such a fraudulent representation might be set up as a defense to an action upon the bill, even at suit of a holder of the bill for value before maturity, and without notice of the fraud. The indorsement under these latter circumstances might be invalidated not merely on the ground of fraud, but on the ground that the mind of the alleged indorser did not accompany his signature—in other words, that he never intended to sign, and therefore in contemplation of law never did sign, the contract to which his name is appended.[59] This mode of looking at a transaction involving fraud is often applicable. A contract induced by fraud, if the objection to it be aptly taken, is regarded as void *ab initio*, or as never having had any legal entity.

49. A distinction must, however, at once be noticed between the case where a contract may be rescinded on account of fraud, and the case where it may be rescinded on the ground that there is a difference in substance between the thing bargained for and that obtained. As regards the former state of things, it is enough to show that there was a fraudulent representation as to any part of that which induced the party to enter into the contract sought to be rescinded. But an innocent misrepresentation or misapprehension as to the subject matter of sale does not authorize a rescission unless there be a complete difference in substance between what was supposed to be, and what was got, so as to constitute a failure of consideration. For exam-

ple, where a horse is bought under a belief that it is sound, if the purchaser was induced to buy by a fraudulent representation as to the horse's soundness, the contract may be rescinded. If the purchaser was induced to buy the horse by an honest representation as to its soundness, the purchaser must pay the price, unless there was a warranty, and even if there were a warranty he could not return the horse and claim back the whole price, unless there were a condition to that effect in the contract.⁽ᵃ⁾

50. In general a contract framed in violation of the unwritten or of the statute law cannot be enforced. No action can be maintained upon it if the defense of illegality be put forward in the proper manner. And should a contract impugned as infringing the principles of our unwritten or customary law be really infected with such a vice, it cannot lay the foundation for an action—cannot if challenged be recognized by a court of law—cannot, in short, give to either contracting party any legal right or impose upon him any legal obligation. A. agrees to let to B. a lecture-room for hire, but before it has been used by B. ascertains that lectures of a blasphemous nature or of an immoral tendency are to be delivered there. A. will be justified in breaking off and rescinding his engagement and in

refusing to allow the room to be used for the purpose named.[61] A plaintiff, moreover, suing to recover money, who cannot present his case to the jury without disclosing the unlawful purpose in furtherance of which the money was paid would be precluded from recovering it in an action.[62]

51. Let us suppose an agreement between A. and B., whereby A. agrees to serve as a seaman on board a ship of which B. is master, for a defined period, on a voyage from London to the foreign port and back to a final port of discharge, at monthly wages. Suppose that on arriving at the foreign port B. purposes making another voyage within the terms of the agreement, but which would either be illegal, regard being had to the foreign enlistment act (59 Geo. III, c. 69), or would at all events expose the ship's crew to personal risk of capture or otherwise, for breach of neutrality, at the hands of a belligerent power in amity with our crown. Would A., when cognizant of the facts and of the purpose of B., be justified in treating the agreement as having been broken and put an end to by him, in quitting the ship and suing B. for breach of contract? A. would seem to be so entitled upon this intelligible ground, that B.'s undertaking really was to employ the crew for a specified period on board his vessel upon an ordinary commercial

voyage, not upon a voyage such as projected, which would expose the crew to greater danger than they had anticipated and bargained for.[63] Here the *onus* of proof would be on A., and, the illegal act proposed or contemplated by B. having been established, a question of law would arise for the judge's decision—was A. thus justified in treating as rescinded the original contract between himself and B.? If so, a further question, by no means free from difficulty, would be as to the amount of damages to be awarded, B., the defendant, being answerable only as *causa causans*, and for such damage alone as naturally, or as has sometimes been said "inevitably," resulted from his wrongful conduct.

52. The reason why evidence is admissible of fraud or illegality attending or inducing to the execution of a contract is this: such evidence goes to show that the alleged contract never had any existence in legal contemplation. There is a semblance merely of a contract, the substance of which disappears by reason of the fraud or illegality vitiating it. This idea should be quite familiar to the mind of one who concerns himself with the law of contracts. It enables him to appreciate the important difference between a defense grounded upon matter posterior to the creation of a contract, and

a defense grounded upon matter contemporaneous therewith, or perhaps antecedent and inducing to it.

53. Quite irrespective of cases involving fraud or illegality, in the sense in which those words are ordinarily used, many contracts might be specified, open to objection as opposed to public policy, to those considerations of a theoretical expediency, hard to be defined, by which our law is sometimes guided. The doctrine referred to is applicable to every class and subdivision of contract, unwritten or written.

"The principle upon which courts of justice must go is to enforce the performance of contracts not injurious to society, and it would be absurd to say that a court of justice shall be bound to enforce contracts injurious to and against the public good." [64] When accordingly the validity of a contract is questioned upon the ground that it is in restraint of trade, which is favored and encouraged by the law, we find that our courts, administering the law with a view to public expediency, have declined to sanction any such contract where the restraint which it aims at enforcing is unreasonable; and as an element in the inquiry whether such restraint is reasonable or not, even where the contract is under seal (Chap. IV), our courts will look for some consideration

(Art. 25) to support the undertaking to abstain from exercising the particular trade; and if no such consideration be found, the contract will be held invalid as unreasonable.[65]

A case of some interest falling within this part of my subject recently occurred. It concerned what are known as voting charities. A. and B. being subscribers to any such charity, and entitled to an equal number of votes at the election of a candidate, thus agree: If A. will give his votes in favor of B.'s candidate on this occasion, B. will vote for A.'s candidate at the next election. Such an agreement was held not to be illegal as opposed to public policy, and an action will lie for breach of it.[66]

54. Matter set forth in the preceding pages may have enabled us now to answer the question— What is a contract? It is an agreement between parties, containing certain ingredients, of which one or another may sometimes be with difficulty discerned. A contract involves privity and consent, though not necessarily mutuality or reciprocity of obligation.

A contract may be express, evidenced by writing or by words, or implied either from the words used or from the conduct of the principals. Legal principles, however familiar in actions grounded upon express, will be just as available in actions grounded upon implied contracts. Effect will, if possible, be given to the intention of the parties. Fraud inducing to a contract, illegality at the very root of it, public policy violated by and protesting against it, to say nothing of other grounds of objection less general and more technical in their nature, may be set up by way of defense to an action founded upon an implied, as they may set up in an action founded upon an express contract. Indeed, it may be said to follow *a fortiori* that since fraud or illegality—using this latter term in its broadest sense—will vitiate and nullify an express contract, the law will out of a transaction based in and contaminated by fraud or illegality decline to imply a contract, promise, or undertaking.

CHAPTER III.

MERCANTILE CONTRACTS.

" Le commerce, tel que la jurisprudence peut le considérer consiste, dans les diverses négociations qui ont pour objet d'opérer ou de faciliter les échanges des produits de la nature ou de l'industrie, à l'effet d'en tirer quelque profit. Le droit commercial se compose de toutes les règles relatives à la validité et à l'effet de ces négociations, ainsi qu'à la manière de juger les contestations qui peuvent en résulter."—PARDESSUS.

"The custom or law of merchants is part of the common law of this kingdom, of which the judges ought to take notice."—BEAWES.

"The mercantile law of this country is founded upon principles of equity."—Mr. JUSTICE BULLER.

LORD MANSFIELD held "the law to be best applied when made subservient to the honesty of a case."

55. IN the preceding chapter a simple contract has been treated of quite generally; its nature and attributes as well as the ingredients in it having been illustrated by reference indifferently to non-mercantile and mercantile contracts. The law merchant, however, although governed by principles identical with those already indicated, stands somewhat apart from our municipal law applicable to non-traders, and in the following pages will be so regarded.

56. A mercantile contract is, in truth, a contract between mercantile persons relating to mercantile matters, and in it we look for the request,

consideration, and promise already spoken of (Arts. 22-27). The request perhaps may be deducible from the correspondence between the parties. A. negociates with B. for the place of foreman in some department of his business, or for the place of salesman, and the negociation is arranged. A. having taken the place, and performed for a time its duties, is compelled to sue B. for non-payment of his salary. The matter may be looked at thus: the request would be by B. to A. to enter his service, the consideration would consist in the acceptance of the place and performance of its duties by A., the promise would be by B. to pay the salary.

57. The consideration in a mercantile contract, though always to be found there, is sometimes peculiar. If A., having no authority to act as agent for B., assumes to do so, he will be held impliedly to warrant that he has authority, and may incur liability for breach of this implied undertaking to plaintiff. The confidence induced by A. would be a sufficient consideration moving or proceeding from plaintiff to support A.'s promise or undertaking that he had authority to contract. "By the law of England, persons who induce others to act on the supposition that they have authority to enter into a binding contract on behalf of third persons, on it turning out that they have no such

authority, may be sued for damages for the breach of an implied warranty of authority."[67] And so a person professing to practice a particular trade or profession, thereby holds himself out as possessing a reasonable degree of skill in that trade or profession, and should he be found to have been unreasonably ignorant of it, may incur liability for damage thence resulting to a customer, patient, or client.[68] Here the confidence induced by the professing of skill is a sufficient consideration for the promise to exercise it. (See Arts. 27, 38.)

By analogous reasoning, misconduct in a servant may justify the master in discharging him. A clerk is retained for a year to keep a merchant's books, and impliedly undertakes and contracts that he is competent to do so. The clerk is found to be ignorant not only of book-keeping, but of arithmetic. Is the merchant bound to continue to employ him during the year? Common sense supplies the answer to this question—he is not. A master has been held justified in dismissing a domestic servant without notice or payment of a month's wages, which is the usual alternative, for disobedience to lawful orders;[69] and a master would seem equally entitled to dismiss without notice a servant who was found grossly incompetent for the work which he had impliedly undertaken to do.[70]

58. Sometimes, where there has been a contract of sale between parties, a question as to consideration arises. In general, where there is a contract by one party to sell an article, and by the other party to pay for it—no time being named—these two acts are meant to be concurrent. The one is the consideration for the other of them, and when the article is handed over, the price agreed on for it should be paid. It may, however, chance that the thing alleged to have been sold was at the time of the sale colorable merely or non-existent; or it may be found that the property in it had, by virtue of some antecedent contract, passed out of the vendor, so that under the alleged sale nothing in truth passed to the so-called purchaser, from whom therefore nothing can be recovered.[71]

59. A failure of consideration may also be where, on a sale of goods, there has been a complete difference in substance between what was supposed to be and what actually was taken by the buyer, there having been no fraud at all in the transaction, but merely an innocent misrepresentation or a misapprehension. In such case a rescission of the contract may be justifiable (Art. 49); and if so, the price paid for the thing in question may be

reclaimed. Much nicety may, however, be needed in discriminating between the case where the subject-matter of the contract is a specific thing which the buyer is to take, subject to all faults and imperfections, and the case where the subject-matter of the contract is a chattel not specific, but referable to a general class of chattels, and understood to possess the qualities attributable to chattels of such or such a designation.[72] The test here applicable for determining the right of the purchaser to dispute the sale is indicated by the question— Has he got what he bargained for and meant to buy?

60. In a mercantile as in a non-mercantile contract (Arts. 31, 36), the promise, if express, should be definite. The terms of the contract must be complete, not inchoate merely, and must have been assented to by both the contracting parties. Their assent must have been *ad idem*.[73] A. says to B., "If you will give me an order for so much iron or other merchandise, I will supply it at a given price." When the order is given there is a complete contract, which the seller is bound to perform, the request being implied in the words used, and there being an ample consideration for the promise.[74]

61. On the facts just put, the existence of privity (Art. 28) is quite apparent, and from the rule

requiring it as essential to a valid contract, results important to the trading portion of the community may sometimes be deduced. Thus, if a factor or agent intrusted with goods for sale, sells them as his own, and the buyer knows nothing of any principal, the buyer may set off a demand he has on the factor against the demand for the price of the goods made by the principal. In such a state of things, the actual privity is between the buyer of the goods and the factor; and although the real principal may step in and claim the price of the goods, it would be very hard should the buyer be debarred from asserting his cross-claim as against that party with whom he was in actual—ostensible—privity, viz., the factor. The rule stated is practically applied in accordance with principles of natural equity,[75] and in connection with it may be mentioned another rule—that where an agent is the purchaser of goods, and the vendor has given credit to such agent, believing him to be the principal, the vendor cannot recover against the undisclosed principal, if the principal has *bona fide* paid the agent at a time when the vendor still gave credit to the agent, and knew of no one else as principal.[76] Here the actual —ostensible—privity is between the vendor and the agent, and it would manifestly be inequitable to hold the unknown principal liable to pay a second time over for the goods, credit having been given by the vendor to the agent, with whom alone he had treated.

62. If a firm of merchants resident abroad instructs a home firm to purchase goods to be sent out on the joint account of the two firms, this will not *per se* empower the home firm to establish any privity between the vendor here and the house abroad, the presumption being that the foreign principal does not intend that the agent employed here should make him a party to the contract of purchase. Therefore, on the ground of want of privity, no action would lie at suit of the vendor of the goods in this country against the foreign firm." This presumption, when it exists, is deducible from a well-understood course of dealing amongst merchants, which is founded on convenience and on something like necessity—for how can the foreign firm be sufficiently informed as to the solvency, respectability, and trustworthiness of those who sell goods to their home agents or correspondents? Consequently, the home agents have no implied authority to create privity as between their principal abroad and the vendors of goods here.

63. The doctrine of privity may thus properly be applied to test the completeness and efficiency

of a contract made between traders, and having reference to a matter purely mercantile. The test of mutuality or reciprocity of obligation (Art. 92) cannot always be so applied. The contract of suretyship exemplifies this remark. A. guarantees the price of goods to be supplied by B. to C. on the contingency of C.'s default in paying for them. A. thus accepts a possible liability, but B. does not bind himself to supply the goods. This is a very common state of things in practice, though B.'s position would of course be different should there be evidence of an undertaking by him, express or implied, to forward goods to C.

64. The intention of parties to a mercantile contract, when clearly discoverable, may affect their *primâ facie* contract, or may afford a clue for interpreting it. In most cases the intention of parties is sufficiently expressed. If so, should their contract in no way contravene the law, effect must needs be given to it. In the articles which immediately follow, various instances are given of what is said.

65. A question such as just referred to may arise upon a charter-party—a charter-party being "a contract by which an entire ship, or some principal part thereof, is let to a merchant for the conveyance of goods on a determined voyage to one or

more places."[76] Such an instrument, we will suppose, contains an agreement that the ship shall take in a full cargo and proceed to some foreign port, and there, or so near thereto as she may safely get, deliver the cargo in the usual and customary manner, restraints of princes and so forth excepted. From such words may be implied a contract of this kind: That the shipowner and charterer will each use reasonable diligence in performing that part of the delivery which by the custom of the port falls upon him. If the charterers are prevented by the authorities abroad from sending lighters to the ship, as they otherwise must have done, to land the cargo, the shipowner could not sue the charterers for the delay thereby caused, the whole process of landing having been thus rendered impracticable by a cause over which neither party had control.[79] In such a case the object is to deduce from words used the intention of the parties how to act and conduct themselves under a state of facts which had not been contemplated by them when contracting.

66. If there be an agreement to deliver goods to a purchaser on a certain condition which, without default on the part of the vendor, never comes to pass, the latter will not be liable for non-delivery of the goods. But where the agreement is absolute or conditioned on an event which happens, the vendor

will be liable for a breach of the agreement to deliver, although he could not help the non-performance; for he must blame his own heedlessness if he runs the risk of undertaking to perform an impossibility, when he might have provided against it by his contract.[50]

Should there be a contract by A. to sell to B. 200 tons of potatoes about to be sown on specific land of A., there is in such contract an implied understanding or condition that when the time for delivery comes the article contracted for should be in existence—so that if the crop fail without default of the vendor, he may be excused from delivering the entire number of tons contracted for.[81] Here a state of things has occurred which neither of the contracting parties thought of or provided for, and the court is therefore called on to complete, as it were, their original agreement by adapting it specifically to what has actually happened. The agreement thus completed is not, however, inconsistent with that first framed and *pro tanto* acted on. It is quite likely that if the parties had possessed foresight they would have introduced into their contract a term such as was afterwards added to it.

67. If goods are sold to be delivered by installments and paid for accordingly, and the buyer makes default in paying for one installment, under

circumstances such that the seller may reasonably believe that the buyer cannot pay for the goods tendered, and does not mean to go on with the contract, the seller is justified in repudiating it.[62] Cases of this kind seem to be increasing in number, and involve considerations of much practical importance. The policy of the law clearly is to keep parties to their contracts and engagements; yet the hardship would be great in compelling a vendor to continue to supply goods which the purchaser has shown a disinclination to accept an an inability to pay for. Under such circumstances the intention of the parties will be taken to be that their contract is rescinded.

68. Where a bill of lading, or receipt by the master of a ship for goods sent on board for conveyance, and a bill of exchange to cover the goods included in the bill of lading are sent in a letter to a vendee of the goods, it is well understood amongst merchants that the bill of exchange must be accepted, or the bill of lading cannot be retained; and if the bill of exchange be not accepted, but the bill of lading is retained, the bill of lading thus acquired gives no right of property to the person so acquiring it.[53] The presumable intention of the party consigning to act in accordance with this

usage may be modified, but the burden of proof will be on the consignee.

69. A presumption of law may be inoperative, in view of the avowed intention of parties whom it might have affected. Such a presumption is that where items in respect of various transactions appear on the debit side of an account, the items on the credit side of the same account are to be appropriated to the items of debit in order of date, in the absence of other appropriation; but this presumption will be rebutted by evidence showing that such could not have been the intention of the parties.[84]

70. Sometimes an implied term may need to be added to, grafted on, or imported into a contract, with a view to effectuating the intention of the parties to it. And on the solution of the question whether or not it be so may depend their respective rights and liabilities. Where, for instance, tenders are invited for the performance of work in accordance with certain plans and specifications, the question may arise—Is there any implied undertaking, warranty, or guaranty that the work can be done as described in the plans and specifications? Or must the parties tendering satisfy themselves independently in regard to this particular?[85]

71. As a new term or condition may sometimes

be imported into a contract on considerations of convenience and necessity, so may authority to do this or that thing occasionally be implied on the ground of necessity, where otherwise there would be no sufficient authority, and such power, when duly exercised, may impose liability on that person who is presumed in law to have conferred it. Thus, the captain of a ship under certain circumstances may pledge his owner's credit for goods supplied to the ship at the port where she may be lying. The captain, however, has authority to bind the owners to pay for supplies or to repay money advanced only where the necessity of the case gives him that authority. It must appear that the money borrowed was needed, or that the goods supplied were necessary for the use of the ship, and that it was reasonably necessary that the captain should obtain or order them on the owner's credit. If the shipowner were himself at the port in question, or had there an agent authorized and ready to supply the ship's requirements, the captain would have no implied authority to pledge the owner's credit for a purpose such as supposed.[86] The special power thus vested in the captain of a ship, and exercisable as aforesaid, is distinguishable from that general discretionary power with which an agent is often clothed to act for the interests of his principal in emergencies as best he may.

72. Great weight is allowed by our law to mercantile usage, and such a usage when once established is afterwards taken notice of by the courts without formal proof of it.[87] What is a usage recognized among merchants—what is its extent—what does it mean—must be ascertained by evidence. But when once ascertained, the legal effect of the usage upon the contract is matter of law, as also is its reasonableness, certainty, or legality. "The universality of a usage voluntarily adopted between buyers and sellers is conclusive proof of its being in accordance with public convenience."[88]

73. Mercantile usage may operate on a contract in various ways. 1st. By interpreting after a peculiar fashion some word or phrase occurring in it; 2dly. By adding a term to the contract; 3dly. As possessing inherent authority to which the contracting parties may appeal, and by which they may expressly agree that their words shall, if found ambiguous, be explained or their intention be determined.

74. 1st. Mercantile usage may operate on a contract by affixing a meaning to some phrase or word in it. Thus on a sale of goods the invoice expressed

that they should be paid for in "from six to eight weeks." The sale having taken place on the 1st of May, the action was commenced June 18th following, barely seven weeks after the date of sale. Had the action been prematurely brought? that is to say, brought before a complete cause of action had arisen? The jury being called on at Nisi Prius to determine the mercantile meaning of the phrase, "from six to eight weeks," found that the action had not been brought too soon. Such a case—not altogether free from difficulty—may be thus explained. The words used are grammatically meaningless, therefore the jury, as men familiar with trading transactions, were to say whether the time of payment for the goods was to be fairly between the two extremes specified, viz., between six and eight weeks from May 1st; if so, was the 18th of June the fair mean?[89] It was not the province of the judge at Nisi Prius to interpret the phrase here in question, for how could he do so unaided by the testimony of witnesses conversant with the usages of merchants? Such proofs being adduced, it was for the jury, looking at the expression used, to decide the question whether the action had been prematurely brought.

Where goods are consigned in a general ship by a bill of lading to a particular port, "the shipowner's liability for the goods to cease on delivery," such delivery is to be made according to the usage which prevails at the said port. Thus, where goods are to be delivered " at the port of Cardiff," the shipowner's contract is fulfilled if he delivers them at the part of the port where goods of that class are required to be delivered. So, if delivery is by the usage of the port to be made in a certain manner, a delivery in that manner satisfies the shipowner's undertaking to deliver at the port, unless there be something in the terms of the contract inconsistent with the usage.[90] In any such case the true meaning of the contract to carry is ultimately arrived at by evidence of local usage.

75. 2dly. By mercantile usage a term may be added to a contract. The relation of master and servant, existing amongst non-traders as well as traders, will aid in exemplifying what is said. The ordinary rule being that a master is responsible for the act of his servant done within the ordinary scope of his duty, a restriction has been put upon it of this kind—the rule does not apply to sustain a demand made by a servant upon his master, by a workman upon his employer, in respect of damage resulting from the carelessness of a fellow-servant or fellow-workman, where the servants respectively causing and suffering the hurt are engaged in a com-

mon work or employment, in the discharge of a common duty, and under one common control or supervision.⁹¹ The reason of this restriction of the general rule is that the contract creating the relation of master and servant tacitly includes an undertaking by the servant that he will, in consideration of the wages specified, incur and submit himself to the risks ordinarily incident to the course of employment upon which he is about to enter. The liability of the master is thus limited by the terms and nature of the contract between himself and the injured person.

The principle on which this rule rests as to the non-liability of the master for a personal hurt done to his servant by a fellow-servant engaged in one common employment, has been applied to many cases where the immediate object on which the one servant is employed is dissimilar from that on which the other is employed, and yet where the risk of injury from the negligence of the one is so much a natural and necessary consequence of the employment which the other accepts, that it must be included in the risks which are to be considered in his wages. Thus, whenever the employment is such as necessarily to bring the person accepting it into contact with the traffic of a line of railway, risk of injury from the carelessness of those managing that traffic is one of the risks necessarily and naturally incident to such an employment, and is therefore within the operation of the rule.[92]

Before perplexing ourselves with the distinctions just noticed—which are sometimes rather fine—we should make sure that the party sought to be charged really stood in the relation of master towards complainant and him who did the injury. Perhaps some other person was master at the time.[93]

Cases such as cited in this article serve to show that usage may import into a contract some specific term to which nothing at all similar or akin is there found. Nor does it signify whether the term be thus imported directly by the usage, or whether it be imported on analyzing the relation subsisting between parties as explained and elucidated by long continued custom. Looked at in either light, we have before us a contract materially added to by usage, and such a contract as spoken of far more frequently than not falls within the list or catalogue of mercantile contracts.

76. 3dly. A mercantile usage may have inherent authority to which the contracting parties may appeal, and by which they may agree that their words shall, if found ambiguous, be explained, or their intention be ascertained. Mercantile usage may essentially differ from the customary law of

England, and it is competent to persons to exclude the operation of the latter by the express wording of their contract, and to agree to be bound by the former. In any such case the usage appealed to, if existent and valid, will regulate the contract."

Where goods are bought and at once paid for by check, such payment is *primâ facie* conditional only, becoming absolute when the check is honored, or when the holder by his negligent conduct or *laches* makes the check his own. Hence the question—Does a check operate as payment? may depend on this further question—Was it duly presented? and this question may have to be answered by reference to mercantile usage. A check drawn in London on a Jersey banker is accounted a foreign check, and by the custom of London bankers any such banker, when a foreign check is paid to him by a customer, if he has an agent at the place where the check is payable, sends the check to his agent there to be presented for payment. If the London banker has no agent at such place, he sends the check direct by post to the bank whereon it is drawn, and that bank immediately remits the money or returns the check. Should this usage be conformed to on behalf of the recipient of the check, he will not be deemed to have made it his own by *laches*, and, in the event of failure of the foreign bank, will be entitled to recover the price of the goods as against the purchaser.[95]

77. It has been thought well in this chapter to enter at some length into the nature and effects of mercantile usages, as giving a peculiar complexion to that branch of law here treated of, viz., the Law Merchant. In reference to these usages recently reported cases have been cited, a mere glance at some of which will show how great the difficulty may be in interpreting and giving its proper effect to a usage or custom recognized amongst traders, to a word or phrase familiar to them, or in reconciling a usage proved to exist, with the express wording of a contract. Whilst trying to give effect to the intention of parties by incorporating a usage with their contract, the words which they have adopted must first be looked at, and the intention, if thereby clearly expressed, will guide the court.

78. A contract, being grounded on consent, will be vitiated by fraud practiced on the contractor (Art. 48), and the word "fraud" has in mercantile law a very wide significance. Our law merchant regards with jealousy anything at all savoring of bad faith, and where a contract has been made will sometimes absolve from his engagement that party to it whose position has been prejudiced by an act

of the other contracting party, done without his consent or knowledge.

For instance, in an action substantially founded upon or arising out of an alleged sale of goods, such a question as this may arise: Had the purchaser a right to treat the supposed contract of sale as null, or to rescind it? To such a question the answer will be: Where the contract has been induced by misrepresentation, the thing sold under it and delivered may, whilst it retains unaltered its original form and condition, be returned, and the price paid for it may be reclaimed by the vendee; and even where the condition of the chattel has become changed, perhaps even deteriorated—whilst in the vendee's possession, but without his default, as by the act of God or by unavoidable accident—a right to rescind the contract of sale may be insisted on.[96]

The phrase "act of God" just used is applicable where the damage or loss in question has been caused exclusively by such a direct, violent, sudden, and irresistible act of nature as could not by any amount of ability have been foreseen, or, if foreseen, by any amount of care and skill been prevented or resisted.[97]

79. From what has been said in the preceding article, it must not be inferred that a contract of sale can be avoided and treated as null merely be-

cause the vendor has tacitly suffered and acquiesced in the self-deception of the buyer; such conduct, albeit reprehensible, would not be tantamount to active and express fraud.[98]

80. Our law, however, tries to enforce good faith—not merely to repress gross fraud—in dealings between traders, *ex. gr.*, in the case of a marine policy of insurance as between the assured and the underwriters the utmost good faith is required, so that a concealment or withholding by the assured of material facts which ought to be known by and therefore disclosed to the underwriter, will vitiate the policy.[99]

From the sensitiveness of our law in regard to the observance of good faith by contracting parties, difficulty has sometimes arisen. Thus, it is well established that a principal—although civilly liable for the misfeasance of his agent in the course of his employment as such—is not liable for the wrongful act of his agent in any matter beyond the scope of the agency, unless he (the principal) has expressly authorized it to be done, or has subsequently adopted it for his own use and benefit.[100] Is, then, a principal who has had the benefit of a contract made by his agent responsible for a deliberate fraud committed by such agent in the making of the con-contract—by which fraud alone the contract was effected? Is a principal liable for a fraud committed by an agent employed in the ordinary course of his business? Can the consequences of fraud in an agent be fixed upon a man morally innocent as regards it? On the other hand, is a customer of the principal, dealing and negotiating with his accredited agent, necessitated to look to the agent personally and exclusively for damages caused by his fraud in the regular course of business, and so, perhaps, to be practically without redress?

The distinction between what is called moral and what is called legal fraud has caused much perplexity. Can there be in contemplation of law conduct which will entail the consequences of fraud, without any ingredient of moral turpitude? In the language of pleading, a master is said to do an act by his servant—a principal is said to do an act by his agent. Can the master or the principal properly be said to commit a fraud—*ex. gr.*, to make a false representation by his servant or agent, who has no express authority to do what is wrongful—so as to be made civilly responsible for its consequences?[101] Can a case such as put be likened to, or is it to be distinguished from, that ordinarily occurring, in which a principal is held to be affected by the statement or admission of his agent made in the regular course of his employment? Could the fraudulent misstatement of the agent be considered as made at all within the scope of his duty, and in the character of agent?

Again, can the liability of the master or principal, in any case such as above put, be regarded as analogous to that of a member of a partnership, who may, under certain circumstances, be answerable for the delinquency of his copartner, causing loss of money to a third person. For instance, the plaintiffs, who were executors and trustees under a will, employed A. and B., a firm of solicitors, to procure investments for the assets of their testator. Plaintiffs' dealings were with A., who, having received money from them to be advanced on mortgage, paid it nevertheless into a bank to the partnership account, representing to plaintiffs that it had been applied as they directed. A. having for many years paid interest regularly in respect of the pretended mortgage, dissolved partnership with B., and afterwards became bankrupt. Then plaintiffs first became aware of A.'s default, and were held entitled to full relief as against B.—B., though morally innocent, being civilly liable for the fraud of his copartner. Although, in the case presented, the relief was sought in equity, the ground of the decision, and the reasoning on which it was based, would be recognized in a court of law—viz., that the act of one partner, done in regard to the regular business of the firm, is binding on his copartner, even if such act consist in a fraudulent misrepresentation made by the partner when transacting the partnership business.[102]

The answer to any question put in the three preceding paragraphs could only be given after careful consideration of the facts submitted. It may well be that a principal would be liable in respect of the misrepresentation of an agent contracting or assuming to contract on his behalf, yet not liable for fraud of the agent, entirely isolated from contract, causing damage. To this aspect of the inquiry I shall advert in the ensuing chapter.

81. Illegality may afford ground of defense to an action on a mercantile as on a non-mercantile contract. For instance, it is generally true that a plaintiff suing for work and labor done in contravention of the common or statute law cannot recover for it, nor can a plaintiff successfully rely upon defendant's promise to reimburse him for money paid or damage incurred under a corrupt agreement—our law declining to lend aid to one who has thus aimed at violating its provisions.[103] So an agreement executed with a view to the doing of an illegal act—and so executed under a sort of compulsion, and not by one who can be

regarded as a free agent—will not be enforced in equity, and the principle involved in this decision is just as applicable at law.[104] So where a chattel has been pledged—the absolute property therein remaining in the pledgor or person pledging it, the special property being in the pledgee—and the original deposit was made in respect of an illegal transaction, to which both pledgor and pledgee were privy—if the pledgor suing for the chattel cannot make out his right to it without showing the true character of the deposit, he will be precluded from obtaining the assistance of the law for getting back the chattel,[105] because the law will not at all lend its aid to enforce compensation for breach of an illegal compact.

82. Clearly, then, where a contract is to do a thing which cannot be done without violation of the law, such contract may be avoided. But in order to avoid a contract which can be legally performed, on the ground that there was an intention to perform it in an illegal manner, it is necessary to show that there was a wicked intention to break the law.[106]

In connection however with this part of our subject the question sometimes arises: Where is the line to be drawn between an act done in violation and an act done in evasion of a statute?

An agreement to contravene an act of Parliament, *i. e.*, pointing and leading to a contravention of it, would be illegal, and yet an arrangement meant to evade an act, perhaps to escape from revenue burdens, might not necessarily be so. The expression that something done was "a fraud upon a statute" is familiar; it applies, for instance, to an attempt made to deceive and defraud creditors in breach, not of the words, may be, but of the spirit and policy of the bankrupt law. The expression cited should, however, be used with due discrimination. The Legislature may designedly or *per incuriam* omit to provide against every imaginable state of things, and under special circumstances it may be found that the mischief intended to be prevented by its enactment has not been prevented. Therefore, assuming that the terms of the particular act have been complied with, a lawyer may well hesitate to characterize as illegal what has been done, or to say that the agreement out of which it originated was either voidable or void.[107] It may also be very necessary to restrict within reasonable limits the operation of a statute affixing the character of illegality to an act or omission, *ex. gr.*, where the object of an act of Parliament is to prohibit a voyage. The illegality attaching to the voyage attaches also to the policy of insurance covering the voyage, but where passengers are taken by the master of a vessel without her owner's knowledge, no certificate having been obtained enabling the vessel to carry passengers, this illegal conduct of the master will not, it seems, vitiate a policy on the ship effected by her innocent owner.[108]

83. From what has been set forth in this chapter, we infer that a mercantile contract—though governed generally by rules applicable to contracts between non-traders—is more liable than they are to be affected by usage, and that in regard to a mercantile contract the nicest good faith must be observed. The language of traders, moreover, is peculiar, and likely to cause embarrassment to persons not conversant with it; what traders have said and written, accordingly, may need to be explained by experts, or at all events by those familiar with their dealings. Our courts, without undue indulgence, will decline to fetter merchants in their transactions with each other, and will abstain from so interpreting an act of Parliament, if this be possible consistently with its meaning, as to nullify or render illegal their arrangements.

CHAPTER IV.

WRITTEN INSTRUMENTS.

> "Delere licebit
> Quod non edideris; nescit vox missa reverti."—Hor.
> "Vox audita perit, litera scripta manet."—Anon.
> "Scripta ferunt annos."—Ovid.

84. The object of this chapter is to put before the reader some practical remarks as to contracts or agreements evidenced by writing, which are divisible into three classes, viz.: simple contracts which are in writing, though not required to be so; simple contracts which must be in writing, whether by virtue of the statute or by force of the customary law; and deeds.

85. As regards the class of contracts first mentioned, something has been from time to time incidentally said. The fact that an agreement between parties has been committed to writing affects the mode of proving it rather than its significance or efficacy. Our law indeed requires that a fact be proved at the trial of a cause by the best or highest kind of evidence which the nature of the case admits of, and evidence such as implies that

better proof is attainable, being secondary only, cannot be received. This rule is necessarily subject to exceptions—as where the best evidence has been destroyed or lost, or is in the possession of the adverse party, who, after due notice, refuses to produce it.

Let us suppose an action to be brought upon a contract, and that it appears at the trial from parol evidence that the contract declared on has been put into writing by the parties to it, that writing being the best evidence of the contract must, if possible, be produced; and it will be for the judge to say whether the existence of a written contract between the litigating parties embodying the verbal contract sued upon be sufficiently proved to entitle the defendant's counsel to call for its production, or whether sufficient proof has been adduced by the plaintiff that the writing is not in his possession or within his control to let in secondary evidence of its contents. The rule adverted to is founded on a sort of presumption that there is something in the evidence withheld which makes against the party who ought or might be expected to produce it. Should such evidence, however, be shown to be unattainable, this presumption ceases, and the inferior kind of proof is admissible. If, therefore, the original of a writing needed as proof in a cause be shown to be in the possession of the adverse party, and be not after notice produced by him, or be shown to have been lost or destroyed, secondary evidence of its contents may be given; and if the writing be in the possession of a third person who is not by law compellable to produce it, and he refuses to do so, the result is the same, for the original is then unattainable by the party offering the secondary evidence.

86. From what precedes, it logically follows that verbal statements made contemporaneously with the signing of a written agreement by either party to it cannot be received in evidence to vary the terms of the agreement, though parol evidence to show that there had in fact been no agreement at all would be admissible. In an action brought for breach of a written contract, the defense may be that it was never meant to have any effect, or that it was to take effect not absolutely and immediately, as contended for, but conditionally on the happening of an event which has not happened, and either of such matters of defense might be proved by extrinsic parol evidence. Proofs would not, however, be admissible to show that the alleged contract was to have a partial effect. In the former case the agreement would really be

denied altogether; in the latter case the evidence proffered would go to vary the written contract.[109]

87. It is for the judge to construe a written contract, and there may be great difficulty in doing so; it is sometimes hard to ascertain and unravel the meaning of words, and parties who use language involved or doubtful have themselves to blame should their real intention be misconstrued. "If," for example, "a principal gives an order to an agent in such uncertain terms as to be susceptible of two different meanings, and the agent *bonâ fide* adopts one of them and acts upon it, it is not competent to the principal to repudiate the act as unauthorized because he meant the order to be read in the other sense of which it is equally capable;" the principal ought to have given his order in clear and unambiguous terms,[110] and language, if ambiguous, is to be construed in the sense least favorable to the person using it.

88. Contracts required to be in writing, but not under seal, are constituted by force either of the law merchant or of statutory law. We should look in vain for contracts, unauthenticated by sealing and delivery, which were yet required to be in writing in virtue of our common law non-mercantile. The customary law of England in remote ages recognized the efficacy of a charter or a deed, but

regarded all other contracts falling within the scope of this chapter as of equal force and equal rank. "All contracts are by the laws of England distinguished into agreements by specialty [*i. e.*, deed] and agreements by parol; nor is there any such third class as contracts in writing."[111] However, as trade established itself such contracts were needed, and from time to time the Legislature made writing indispensable to the validity of certain agreements.

89. We may accordingly say that up to the passing of the statute of frauds (29 Car. II, c. 3), every contract was referable either to the class of special or to that of simple contracts—that the latter of these two classes was not subdivisible, except where, as in the case of bills of exchange, mercantile convenience had necessitated a recourse to writing by contracting parties. Since the statute of frauds, other statutes—pre-eminently Lord Tenterden's act (9 Geo. IV, c. 14), and the series of enactments having reference to corporate bodies, joint stock and public companies—have augmented the list of contracts which must be in writing, these enactments having been passed principally for the benefit and advancement of trade and commerce. Abstaining from a detailed examination of statutory provisions such as adverted to, a few instances will be given showing their practical operation, and

selected with a view to illustrating remarks made respecting simple contracts, their component ingredients and attributes, in the two preceding chapters.

90. A guaranty—a security common amongst merchants—being " a special promise to answer for the debt, default, or miscarriage of another person," must, under sec. 4 of the statute of frauds, be evidenced by some memorandum in writing, signed by the party to be charged on the guaranty, or by his agent thereunto lawfully authorized. A guaranty is unilateral, and to satisfy the statute of frauds and fix the guarantor with liability upon it, there must be either a written contract complete in itself, or a contract in writing on different papers referring to each other in such a manner as to show that they are parts of the same contract, leaving nothing to be supplied by verbal evidence, except the identity of the documents.[112]

91. As showing the nature of a guaranty, its practical use, the relation between the parties to it, the remedies available on it, and proofs adducible in aid of them, this state of facts may be supposed: A. asks B. to advance him a sum of money, B. declines to do so unless C. will answer for its repayment, and C. accordingly becomes guarantor for A., whereupon B. makes the advance asked for. As between A. and B. this transaction is a loan, in

which are comprised the request, consideration, and promise, constituting a complete simple contract (Art. 22). A loan cannot be unless at the request of its recipient; the consideration is the sum advanced; and the promise implied by law is to repay it on demand. Should A. make default in doing so, an action for the debt might be brought against him at suit of B. The liability of A. to B. under the above circumstances is direct.

92. Towards B., C. the guarantor, stands in a position different from that occupied by A., upon whose default in repayment of the loan, C. becomes liable to B. in an action upon the guaranty. To support such action, in the absence of any admission, the guaranty must be produced at the trial, and if signed by C., his handwriting must be proved, the consideration for his promise must be shown, and a material question may arise upon the guaranty itself. Is it continuing, or so worded as to be in force for a limited time only, and then to become null?

The consideration for the undertaking to guarantee may be, as above supposed, an immediate advance of money, or the giving of credit *in futuro*, or the forbearing to sue in respect of an accrued debt, or the employment of A. by B. in his service, and so forth. The consideration must not, however, be wholly past and executed when the promise is made, though it may be in part executed and in part executory. The consideration need not now, in virtue of a modern statute,[113] be set forth in or appear by necessary implication from the guaranty.

. The position of C. in reference to B. is thus peculiar: there is an absence of mutuality in the contract (Art. 63). B. says to C.: I may possibly supply goods to A., but shall not do so unless you will guarantee payment for them. This arrangement, when sufficiently evidenced by writing, is at once binding upon C., yet B. may decline to supply the goods, and no action would lie against him for such refusal. The contract does not impose obligations which are reciprocally enforceable. This feature in the instrument known as a guaranty is worthy of special notice. Negotiations may be carried on with a view to the employment of A. by B. as his cashier, and at length result in or be apparently terminated by the giving of a guaranty by C. that A. shall, if so employed, faithfully make out his accounts and pay over balances to B.; nevertheless, B. may, without incurring liability, capriciously abstain from completing this arrangement.[114]

93. As between A. and C., the parties respectively in favor of whom and by whom the guaranty is given, the state of things is this: C., if compelled to pay on A.'s default, has a remedy against A. by

action for the money so paid, inasmuch as the law implies a promise by the principal to make good to the surety the money which he has been compelled to pay in virtue of his undertaking. So where judgment has been recovered and execution had at suit of the party to whom the guaranty has been given, against one of several co-sureties of the party guaranteed, a promise is likewise implied that each of the other sureties will contribute ratably to make good the damage suffered, and our law defines precisely the nature of this promise, that he will recoup his *aliquot* or ratable share of the entire judgment debt recovered, to the party who has under compulsion paid it.[115]

By stat. 19 & 20 Vict. c. 97, s. 5, a surety who discharges the liability of his principal will be entitled to an assignment of all securities held by the creditor in respect of the debt discharged or duty performed by the surety.

94. Such being in brief the position relatively to each other of the parties to a guaranty, these questions may be entertained: Does a given instrument in truth evidence "a special promise" to answer for the "debt, default, or miscarriage" of a third person? Is it or is it not within the operation of the 4th section of the statute of frauds? The mode of responding to these questions is indi-

cated by others: Is the liability assumed by the so-called guarantor under the instrument, collateral or direct? Does the party owing the debt, or guilty of the default or miscarriage, remain liable in respect thereof? If the liability incurred is collateral, if the party originally liable still remains so, the contract is within the statute. Much difficulty may be felt in distinguishing between a direct and a collateral liability—in determining whether the true character of a person is that of principal or of surety—and such difficulty may have to be determined at Nisi Prius.[116]

95. A further important question arising upon a guaranty may be this: Is it continuing, or is it in force for a limited time only? The language of a guaranty, if thus ambiguous, may however be explained by evidence of extrinsic circumstances and by proof of the relative position of the parties to one another at the time when the instrument was written, the object being to find out their intention, and if possible give effect to it without doing violence to the words which have been used.[117] By reason of the difficulty sometimes felt in construing a guaranty, it was enacted by stat. 19 & 20 Vict. c. 97, s. 4, that a guaranty to or for a firm shall, except in special cases, cease to be in force upon a change in the constitution of the firm.

96. In the contract now spoken of, the nicest good faith is to be looked for, so that not merely fraud but non-disclosure of a material fact may avoid it.[118] If the creditor, without the consent of the surety, by his own act destroy the debt or derogate from the power which the law confers upon the surety to recover it, as against the principal debtor, in case he should have paid it to the creditor, the surety is discharged. Where a surety has agreed to become bound to a master on certain terms for the due performance of duty by his servant, and those terms are afterwards so altered as between the master and servant as to increase the risk of the surety, he would be discharged. Though if the change be in some purely collateral and immaterial point, that would afford no defense to the surety if sued for breach of his contract and undertaking.[119] Should a continuing guaranty however be given for the honesty of a servant, and should the master detect him in dishonesty, if instead of dismissing he choose to retain in his employ a dishonest servant, the surety kept in ignorance of this will cease to be liable on his guaranty.[120]

To an action on a guaranty the defense set up was that after it had been made and delivered to the plaintiff, and whilst in his hands, the instrument had by some person unknown been altered by such person affixing a seal to it, so as to make it purport to have been sealed by the defendant. The alteration here alleged to have been effected in the instrument was obviously material, inasmuch as the properties of a deed are widely different from those of a simple contract, and the court held that the alteration made avoided the guaranty.[121]

97. It might perhaps have been supposed that the state of facts rendering necessary the instrument treated of had been sufficiently defined by the Legislature and by legal tribunals, and that it had been in all respects well cared for by our written and customary law; we have, however, already seen that it is sometimes possible to evade the provisions of a statute (Art. 82, *ad fin.*), and so a practice was initiated and gradually prevailed of shaping the cause of action upon a guaranty, when merely verbal and therefore insufficient to support the action, as upon a fraudulent misrepresentation concerning the solvency and trustworthiness of another, the gist and substance of complaint being thus presented as a wrongful act, rather than as a breach of contract or undertaking. This being so, the Legislature deemed it advisable to interpose and provide specially for the state of facts so imagined and exhibited by the pleader. The 6th section of Lord Tenterden's act (9 Geo. IV, c. 14), re-

quiring a "representation or assurance," such as supposed, to "be made in writing, signed by the party to be charged therewith."

Under this latter statute, points not free from difficulty may arise. A letter is written and signed by J., the manager of a banking company, in answer to an inquiry concerning the credit and solvency of R., put to him by a third party, S. The letter contains misstatements and misrepresentations knowingly made in reference to such matter, and afterwards causing pecuniary loss to S. Upon these facts, apparently so simple, important legal questions may arise. Can the bank manager be regarded in any sense as the bank, so that his false statement is that of the bank? This can hardly be, though the bank might, by adopting his false statement as that of their agent, for their own advantage, estop themselves from afterwards repudiating the agency. If the manager cannot be looked on as identical with the bank, can he be regarded as their agent, in the case put, so as in any way to make them liable for his false representation? The answer is that the manager cannot—even if regarded as agent for the bank in answering the question as to R.'s trustworthiness—thus cast on them responsibility. By Lord Tenterden's act, sec. 6 the signature of the agent will not charge the principal. The personal liability of the manager, in the case put, looking at the finding of the jury, could not be doubted. He had made a false representation as to the solvency and trustworthiness of another person, with intent that such person should obtain credit by it, and had made it in writing, and signed the document.[122] Damage had thus been sustained by the plaintiff, S., and the cause of action was complete (Chap. VII).

98. The 4th section of the statute of frauds applies to some other contracts besides guaranties, and *inter alia* to contracts for the sale of land or any interest therein; and sec. 17 applies to such contracts as concern the sale of goods where the price agreed upon for them is £10 or upwards. To the former class of contracts no further reference can here be made, a contract falling within it usually necessitating, by reason of its importance, forethought and professional advice.

99. The contract for a sale of goods, already more than once adverted to (Arts. 39, 49, 58), has been regulated as well by our unwritten as by our written law, for in very early times this proposition in regard to it was established, that a sale or barter of goods was complete when the price had been agreed upon, provided there had been a delivery of the subject-matter of the sale, or the price had been

paid in part, or earnest had been given and received. In general, moreover, by our customary law, where specific goods are the subject of a contract of immediate sale, the property in them passes to the purchaser upon completion of the bargain, so that the vendor has then a right to recover the price, though this will not be so should there be circumstances whence an intention may be inferred that the property should not at once vest in the purchaser.[123] Here the intention when ascertained is a key for interpreting the contract. The question whether the property in a chattel has or has not passed under a contract of sale may be important; it may need solution for ascertaining on which of the two parties, buyer or seller, the loss should fall, if by fire or other accident the subject-matter contracted about perishes before it has been dealt with —before dominion has been exercised over it by the buyer. The property in the goods or chattel perishes to the *dominus*—but who is he? In whom is the property vested?— for the risk is his.[124]

100. The 17th section of the statute of frauds applies to contracts for the sale of goods where the price agreed upon is £10 or upwards, and, having regard to the requirements of the common law, enacts that if there be no acceptance and actual receipt of the goods sold, or part thereof, nothing

given in earnest to bind the bargain, or in part of payment, there must be some note or memorandum in writing of such bargain made and signed by the party to be charged thereby or his agent. As to the true significance of the words set forth, very many questions have arisen, of which however, regard being had to the aim of this volume, two only will be entertained. What are we to understand by " acceptance and actual receipt " of goods ? The answer to this question may, under ordinary circumstances, be given on reference to the facts in evidence, as shown by the following cases. The defendant, who was a butcher, verbally agreed with the plaintiff to purchase of him some cattle then being in his (the plaintiff's) field. After the bargain was concluded, the defendant, finding that he had not got his check-book with him, told the plaintiff to call at his house in the evening and he should be paid. It was then arranged that the cattle should remain in the plaintiff's field for a few days, and should be fed with the plaintiff's hay by the defendant. This having been done, the defendant afterwards repudiated the bargain, and the question arose—whether there was evidence of an acceptance and a receipt of the cattle within the statute. It was held that no sufficient evidence to this effect appeared; there had been no actual receipt of the cattle by the defendant, and the act of feeding the cattle with the plaintiff's assent could not be deemed an exercise of such an act of ownership as to amount to an acceptance by, and constructive delivery to, the defendant.[125] On the other hand, a receipt and an acceptance were held to have been properly inferred from the following facts: A. (the defendant) agreed to purchase of B. (the plaintiff) a carriage, then standing in B.'s shop; and after some alterations had been made in the carriage by the defendant's order, he requested that it might remain, as in fact it did, on the plaintiff's premises, but the defendant himself made use of it on one occasion. It was argued, in this case, that there had been no delivery to the defendant, nor any acceptance and actual receipt by him of the carriage; the court nevertheless held, that there had been both a sufficient delivery and acceptance of the carriage; that the defendant had dealt with it as his own; and that the plaintiff, in retaining the actual ostensible possession of the carriage, was, under the circumstances, to be regarded as filling the character of a mere agent or warehouseman for the defendant.[126]

Cases akin to the above are often *sub judice*, but where the facts established are not precisely the same, an inference from one such case to another must cautiously be drawn.

101. A sale of goods, then, of the value of £10 or upwards, regard being had to the requirements of the statute of frauds, if contested, is usually proved by writing or by acceptance and actual receipt of the goods, or by part payment for them; and the difficulty in establishing any one of these heads of proof will be in regard to its sufficiency in contemplation of the jury, or will be such as may arise upon the statute.

As matter of law, it has been adjudged that the written contract or memorandum relied on as satisfying the statute, will not suffice, if signed by one of the principal parties as agent for the other—that the signature as agent must be by some third person.[127] Very often it is by a broker or an auctioneer. An auctioneer, for example, acting under due authority, may sign in compliance with the statute of frauds as agent for purchaser of the goods sold. At a public sale of goods, it is usual for him to write down in his sale book, containing a copy of the conditions of sale, the name of the highest bidder as purchaser of any particular lot, and also the amount of the purchase money, opposite to the lot sold. When the auctioneer thus signs for the purchaser, the statute of frauds is satisfied, because there has thus been made a "note or memorandum in writing" of the "bargain," signed by the agent of the vendee. But when the public sale is over, the implied agency of the auctioneer arising from his character and function ceases.[129] In such a case extrinsic evidence will be admitted as to facts necessary for deciding whether the statute has been complied with, and so deciding whether the contract sued upon is, using the statutory word, "good."

102. It may, perhaps, have occurred to the reader that transactions daily take place, involving the sale and purchase of goods above £10 in price, with reference to which the statutory requirements above noticed are disregarded—either party to any such transaction preferring to incur the risk, in event of default on the other side, of being wholly without remedy, rather than the trouble of conforming to the statute. If a person goes into a shop and orders goods without either receiving them at the time or paying for them—the price of such goods exceeding £10—no action could be brought against him for subsequently refusing to accept the goods so ordered and *bonâ fide* deemed to have been sold. And yet such a transaction as this is constantly taking place without apprehension by either party to it, of unpleasant consequences, and even amongst persons engaged in trade, a like disregard of the statutory provisions

is even habitually shown, no memorandum being made on the sale of goods which could successfully be relied on as sufficient.

103. Sometimes, however, as our law reports testify, an objection is taken to the enforcement of an alleged contract, or rather to the demand of damages for its infraction, upon the ground that no sufficient proof of such contract is forthcoming—*ex. gr.*, where a variance occurs between the bought and sold notes issued to his client by a broker—and much apparent hardship may result.[129]

Hence we infer how inexpedient it must be in operations of magnitude either to waive a strict and literal compliance with the statute law which requires certain contracts to be evidenced by writing, or to be anywise remiss in conforming to it. True it is, that doubts respecting the policy which dictated the 17th section of the statute of frauds have sometimes been expressed, but so long as this section remains in force, its provisions must be complied with, or the risk indicated in them must be incurred—the risk, viz., of being defeated in an action brought to recover a just claim arising out of a sale of goods. Nor may such a contract falling within the scope of the said section and committed to writing be varied by verbal proofs on any pretext that its terms may seem to be susceptible of much latitude of construction and interpretation. In general it will be found that the language used amongst mercantile men indicates their meaning sufficiently well if, for its explanation, we avail ourselves of mercantile usage and custom, and the evidence of those conversant with commercial language; and where a purely mercantile word or phrase occurs in a written contract, and its meaning is fixed and ascertained by apt proofs, the contracting parties will not be permitted to vary, whether to enlarge or restrict, that meaning by subsequent verbal stipulations.

Connected with this part of my subject a somewhat curious point was recently decided, viz., that the signature of the promisor or party to be charged under sec. 17 of the statute of frauds may suffice to satisfy its requirements, although the memorandum of agreement to which it was affixed then contained interlineations afterwards struck out, and although the contract itself was not in other respects such as it afterwards became, the purchaser of goods and party to be charged having verbally assented to the terms of the contract as finally arranged. The parol evidence of assent was here admitted, not to vary the written contract, but to show what was the condition of the document when it became a contract between the parties.[130]

104. The 7th section of Lord Tenterden's act (9 Geo. IV, c. 14) extends the provisions of the 17th section of the statute of frauds, which apply specifically to "contracts for the sale of goods, wares, and merchandises for the price of £10 sterling or upwards" to contracts for the sale of goods of that value intended for delivery at some future time, and which may not at the date of the contract be made or be ready for delivery. The effect of this clause of Lord Tenterden's act, taken in conjunction with the 17th section of the statute of frauds, is that contracts for the sale of goods, as well executory as executed, must, save in certain excepted cases—as when earnest is given or part of the purchase money is paid down—be in writing.

Where the contract is for the purchase of goods to be made according to specification, there being no contract in writing—as in such a case there ought to be—between the parties, a remedy by action afterwards contemplated for breach of such contract may perhaps be found unavailable by force of a provision contained in sec. 4 of the statute of frauds, thus far unnoticed, which renders some written memorandum necessary in authentication of a contract "not to be performed within the space of one year from the making thereof." The meaning of these statutory words however is confined to contracts which are not to be carried into execution within the year, and does not extend to such as may by force of circumstances be postponed beyond that period; otherwise it has been said,[131] " there is no contract which might not fall within the statute." Nor is an agreement within the scope of the statutory words which might have been performed within the year, although both parties expected that its performance would last longer than the year.[132]

105. In preceding articles I have shown that a plaintiff may fail at Nisi Prius because he has not come thither provided with the requisite statutory proof of his contract; he may also fail by reason of not having obtained from the defendant some statutory acknowledgment of liability.

Let us suppose an action to be brought for the price of goods, and that the defense meant to be put forward is that the period of six years prescribed by the statute 21 Jac. I, c. 16, as a bar, if aptly insisted on, to such an action, has run since the accrual of the debt; let us further suppose that in answer to this ground of defense is to be set up an acknowledgment of the debt. Such an answer to the defense might by our customary law have been substantiated by proof of a verbal admission or recognition of liability, but by the statute 9 Geo. IV, c. 14, already several times referred to, such an acknowledgment was required to be in writing signed by the debtor, though the operation of this particular provision was extended by section 13 of the mercantile law amendment act (19 and 20 Vict. c. 97) to the case of such an acknowledgment signed by an agent duly authorized to make it. An important qualification, however, of the rule giving efficacy to a promise to pay a debt barred by the statute of James I must be kept in view; if the promise be to pay conditionally, proof must be given of the performance or fulfillment of the condition in order that the promise may suffice to bar the statute. Upon a general acknowledgment a general promise to pay may properly be implied, but where the party guards his acknowledgment, and accompanies it with an express declaration to prevent any such implication, why should not the promisor be understood to mean that he will only pay conditionally? If B. promises to pay his debt to A. when able to do so, some proof of B.'s ability to pay must, in order to fix him with liability, be laid before the jury. In such a case the construction of the document relied upon by plaintiff may be doubtful.[133]

106. The class of written instruments thirdly mentioned in Art. 84, comprises deeds. A definition accordingly may here be proper. "A deed is a writing containing a contract, and signed, sealed,

and delivered by the party."[134] "Know that there are three things necessarily appertaining to a deed, viz., writing, sealing, and delivery."[135] And, strange as it may seem, "To constitute a sealing, neither wax nor wafer nor even an impression is necessary." Neither is any particular form of words or act needed to constitute delivery. The mere affixing the seal does not, indeed, render the instrument a deed, but as soon as there are acts or words sufficient to show that it is intended by the party to be executed as his deed, presently binding on him, that is sufficient.

A deed, being characterized by the solemnities attending its completion, has peculiar efficacy, and some peculiar qualities. It is "the most solemn and authentic act that a man can possibly perform with relation to the disposal of his property."[136] To this instrument applies the maxim that "things of a higher nature determine things of a lower nature."[137] An agreement under seal, or specialty, will merge, *i. e.*, swallow up and annul the remedy in respect of the simple contract so authenticated. It does not in general need any consideration (Arts. 22, 58) to support it, but the evidence of consent in such a contract is forthcoming in the receipt and acceptance of the instrument by either of the contracting parties. Our law, as just stated, requires that a deed shall be delivered actually or constructively, and if so delivered it must be actually or constructively received.

Further, a deed estops or concludes the parties to it from gainsaying what they have thereby asserted, and the force of this estoppel may be such as to preclude a party to it from insisting on the illegality of a transaction between himself and the other party to the instrument.[138] An estoppel, moreover, binds not only the parties but their privies. "If a man make a lease by indenture of D. in which he hath nothing, and after purchases D. in fee, and then bargains and sells it to A. and his heirs, A. shall be bound by this estoppel,"[189] and so would persons be claiming under him.

In another important particular does a deed differ from a simple contract. Upon the latter, in case of the death of the contractor or promisor, the remedy, if any, must be against his personal representatives. A man cannot by simple contract render his heir liable to an action upon it; such action, if maintainable at all, will be so against his executors or administrators. Such is the policy of our common law; it is otherwise in regard to a contract under seal, which is binding on the heir so far as he may have taken real assets by descent.

107. A deed being authenticated by certain solemnities, and containing within it engagements very obligatory and stringent, we may well suppose that apt proof is needed of it at Nisi Prius. In an ordinary action upon a deed, not merely must the instrument be produced, but evidence must be given of its due execution, if put in issue. However, (1) a deed thirty years old, and coming from the proper custody, proves itself; (2) the attesting witnesses to a deed which does not need to be attested, can be dispensed with at the trial, provided the execution of the deed, not having been admitted, can be proved in some other way; (3) the execution of a deed, even where needing attestation, may be admitted expressly or on the pleadings.

108. For rendering a transaction operative, a deed may, in virtue of the statute or of the customary law, be indispensable. The statute of frauds makes it so in certain cases, and so do provisions of the joint stock companies' acts. According to our unwritten law, the gift of a chattel can only be perfected by delivery or by deed;[140] and, subject to various exceptions, a corporation can only contract efficiently under seal. Let us suppose, for instance, that an annuity or pension has to be granted by such a body to an officer retiring from its service.

The annuity, if granted by resolution merely, would be revocable by the corporation; if meant for the life of the annuitant, or for a term certain, the grant should be by deed.[141]

109. Of deeds, the simplest is a bond whereby one person binds himself to another to pay a sum of money, or to do some specified thing, the parties to the instrument being obligor and obligee respectively. A bond may be executed by a principal and by sureties for the due performance by him of the duties of an office. A bond may be made available as a collateral security, and the issuing of bonds and debentures affords to railway and other companies a ready mode of raising capital for carrying on their works.

110. A bond is unilateral. It may be single, *i. e.*, may simply acknowledge a liability to pay money. In practice, however, to the bond is attached a condition framed according to the intentions of the parties, and setting forth terms compliance with which will render the obligatory part of the instrument void and of no effect. Such, indeed, was the strictness of the common law, that an absolute forfeiture of the bond ensued on non-performance of the condition annexed to it, and although courts of law, assimilating their doctrine to that of courts of equity, ultimately relaxed in rigor towards a de-

faulting obligor, it was not until the time of Queen Anne that adequate relief was extended by the Legislature to the obligor of a money bond, who, through inability or remissness, had failed to pay the sum secured by it on the day appointed. The 4 & 5 Anne, c. 16, ss. 12, 13, enacts that payment of the principal sum secured by bond, together with interest upon it, and costs, though made after the day specified, shall satisfy the bond. Also, by a statute of Will. III (8 & 9 Will. III, c. 11, s. 8), damages and costs of suit only are recoverable in an action upon a bond executed by way of security for the performance of covenants (Art. 114) contained in an indenture, the penalty of the bond not being in this case wholly and irretrievably forfeited.

111. The obligation of a bond may be discharged by cancellation, if the instrument be effaced or destroyed with the intent of canceling and nullifying it, or by a release under seal, *i. e.*, by a deed giving up the right of action or claim which has arisen or may arise upon the bond. A distinction is, however, to be observed between the giving of one bond in satisfaction of another not yet due, and the giving a formal release of an instrument under seal, and then substituting for it another similar security; the former transaction could not, at com-

mon law, be successfully insisted on by way of answer to an action upon the original instrument, whereas the latter transaction might be so, for one deed may be discharged by another deed, and a fresh liability may at the same moment be created.[142] This strict rule of our common law might not be favored in equity, but from what has been latterly said, we infer that a person who has bound himself by deed ought to be very wary in perfecting any arrangement for the dissolution of his contract. He should insist on having the bond delivered up to him when the release is executed, and should by no means satisfy himself with a verbal, or even a written agreement in lieu of its relinquishment by the obligee.

112. A release may be in law, as if a female obligee of a bond marries the obligor, or if the obligee appoints the obligor his executor, in either of of which cases the obligation is extinguished.[143] So the obligation of a bond may be excused by the act of God (Art. 78) rendering performance of the condition annexed to it impossible,[144] or by an act of Parliament prohibiting or preventing it.[145] Further, performance of the condition of a bond may be excused by the default of the obligee, as (1) by his absence in those cases where his presence is necessary for the performance of the condition; (2) by his ob-

structing or preventing the performance; (3) by his neglecting to do the first act towards performance, if it is incumbent on him to do it.[146] An obligor, however, will not by his own willful act rendering performance of the condition of the bond impracticable, be absolved or exonerated from the penalty.[147]

113. Besides the rules, more or less technical, which have been enumerated, we must not forget that broad principles applicable to contracts generally apply to a bond. An instrument so stringent even as this, may on the ground of fraud or illegality be successfully impugned—extrinsic facts may be averred against it. If the condition of the bond be for payment of money, evidence will be admissible in an action upon the bond to show that the consideration for such payment was vicious, such evidence not being inconsistent with the condition, but striking at the very contract itself. Nothing is due under such a contract—the alleged debt never existed—the law gives no right of action for it. These remarks hold good where there is fraud inducing to the execution of a bond, or where it was executed for a purpose opposed to the common or the statute law. In any such case it would be strange indeed if the law upheld the contract or refused to allow the defense suggested to appear on the record.[148]

So a bond opposed to public policy, will be

held void, and certain conditions annexed to bonds have been judicially declared to be against law— *ex. gr.*, a condition (1) To do something *malum prohibitum* or *malum in se*, expressions which, though now discarded, are sufficiently intelligible; or (2) To omit the doing of that which is a duty; or (3) To encourage such crimes or omissions as just indicated. Such conditions as these, we read, the law will always, and without any regard to circumstances, defeat, being concerned to remove all temptations and inducements, either to the commission of a crime or to the omission of a duty. But in construing a condition, if there may be a way found out to perform it without a breach of the law, the condition will be held good.[149]

114. In any kind of indenture or agreement under seal, irrespective of the matter to which it relates, covenants may be inserted, nor is any particular form of words necessary to make a covenant, for "Wherever the court can collect from the particular instrument an engagement on the one side to do or not to do something, that amounts to a covenant."[150] Nor is a covenant necessarily directed to the doing of something *in futuro*, it may amount to an undertaking that something has been already done. A covenant is distinguishable from a condition, which is a kind of proviso creat-

ing, enlarging, or defeating an interest upon the happening of a specified event. A condition may indicate a cause of forfeiture or something which must be done before an interest given can fully vest.

115. As in the case of any other instrument, so in that of an indenture, the court will be called on to construe and interpret its language if obscure—will have to seek out the intention of the parties to an express covenant—or, may be, to raise a covenant by implication out of the words used, and so to confer rights and impose liabilities upon parties which do not originate out of the deed. Or the court may be called on to infer or imply a covenant from the use of certain words having a known legal operation, the main object kept in view being to supply defects of expression, and to prevent the evasion of his covenant by the covenantor in consequence of the equivocal wording of the deed; the courts have therefore adopted as a general rule of construction, that ambiguous words or words in *equilibrio* are to be taken most strongly against the covenantor. This rule was on one occasion applied by Lord Kenyon,[151] to fix a tenant with liability for the expense of building a party wall, for the covenants in the lease usually called tenants' covenants seemed to point to this as being the intention of the

parties, and the words in a deed are to be construed most strongly *contra proferentem*.

116. If consistent with the tenor and import of the instrument, a covenant must be read according to its natural grammatical meaning, for thus may effect best be given to the intent of the parties as set forth and indicated by their words, *ex. gr.*: In a separation deed between husband and wife the husband covenanted with trustees to pay them an annuity for his wife's support "during their joint lives and so long as they should live separate and apart." Did the husband's obligation to pay this annuity cease by reason of a subsequent dissolution of the marriage consequent on the wife's misconduct? It was argued that it did so, the deed contemplating a continuance of the relation which gave rise to it; but this argument did not avail, because no express words thus limiting the husband's liability could be found in the deed, nor was there a clear implication therein to the effect contended for.[152]

An important question may arise upon a deed containing covenants of this kind. Is one of such covenants dependent on another of them, or are they to be viewed as independent? The question suggested is not merely technical in its nature. A. covenants with B. that he will go to York. B.

covenants with A. that he will pay him a sum of
money. It may be, upon construction of the deed,
that the going to York is a condition precedent to
the payment of the money, or it may be that these
two acts are altogether independent of each other,
and according as one or the other interpretation is
adopted, so will the cause of complaint shape itself,
and so will the proofs be adduced, arranged, and
marshaled for Nisi Prius.[153]

117. Thus the framing of covenants may be
fraught with difficulty, even when undertaken by
the skilled conveyancer or the experienced solicitor.
For his guidance one primary rule must be had in
view—he will beware of narrowing and limiting
the operation of an express general covenant, of excluding altogether an implied one, by the insertion
in his draft of words aimed at benefiting his client,
but which, instead of doing so, may prejudice him.
Also the practitioner will beware of binding a covenantor by express words or by necessary implication to do that performance of which may afterwards become impossible.

The lessee of coals under an estate covenanted
to raise a certain quantity of coal in each year
during the term, paying royalty for the same at so
much per ton, and covenanting to pay an equal
amount of money as fixed rent, whether the coals

should or should not be raised. The mine having become exhausted during the term, the lessee thereupon contended that the covenant for payment of rent was conditional on the existence of coal to be worked and paid for. It was held, however, that the covenant in question did not carry with it by implication any such condition as suggested, and no such condition being expressed, it was further held that the lessee was liable for rent according to the scale or standard stipulated by the parties, during the continuance of the term. Neither a court of law nor a court of equity would willingly act in disregard of the maxim, that "the law does not compel a man to do what is impossible." Before doing so they must be well assured that the covenant under notice really has the meaning assigned to it by the covenantee.[154]

A covenantor, moreover, will under certain circumstances be favorably regarded, and will be absolved from his positive engagement where justice requires that he should be so. If, for instance, a man covenants to do that which at the time of covenanting might lawfully be done, and an act of Parliament is subsequently passed which renders the doing of the particular thing unlawful, the covenant is repealed or nullified by the act. Cases within the operation of this rule sometimes occur in consequence of war breaking out between two countries having mercantile dealings with each other. Thus a vessel is chartered to go to a distant port, ship a cargo of goods, and return to this country. Whilst on her voyage, war breaks out with the country in which the foreign port is situate. The vessel in consequence cannot ship her cargo, and in this case the charterer is discharged.[155] If a man covenants not to do that which at the time of covenanting might lawfully be done, and a statute afterwards enacted compels him to do it, here also the statute repeals the covenant. But if a man covenants not to do that which at the time of covenanting was unlawful, and an act comes and makes the doing of it lawful, by the passing of such an act the covenant is not repealed.

118. Satisfied that his contract under seal, whether it be a bond or an indenture, will have to be strictly proved, and that every word and phrase contained in it will be justly construed, a person may, in a transaction of moment and allowing of due deliberation, be well advised to resort to such a method of assurance.

CHAPTER V.

LEGAL PRINCIPLES APPLIED TO CONTRACTS.

"The law of England . . . exclusive of positive law enacted by statute, depends upon principles; and these principles run through all the cases, according as the particular circumstances of each have been found to fall within the one or other of them."—LORD MANSFIELD.

119. IN this chapter an attempt will be made to apply legal principles to given facts involving contract, and to show how questions arising upon such facts should be answered. The words of Lord Mansfield, *supra*, will in the following pages be exemplified, and another remark of the same eminent judge will be fully verified: "The law does not consist in particular cases, but in general principles."

That some familiarity with legal principles, and even with law as applicable to this or that state of facts, is desirable, may perhaps have already become apparent to the reader. In the daily routine of life, and, *a fortiori*, in the course of trading transactions, points continually arise upon which immediate decision must be made; any one of us, indeed, may thus be called on to exercise his judgment and discrimination. If some general or popular knowledge of law be, as I humbly conceive it is, desirable for the community, much more is it fitting that particular sections of the public should acquire, as they may do, familiarity with such branches of our law and such legal principles as specially concern and affect themselves. And this remark seems suitable even where there may be no necessity for coming to an immediate decision as to what should be done in an emergency; a client availing himself of professional aid should have some tolerably definite idea of his actual position, and should be able readily to appreciate, when explained to him, the difficulties surrounding it.

120. In preceding pages the contract of suretyship has been noticed; it is sometimes constituted by deed, sometimes by writing not under seal (Art. 90), and in regard to it an additional remark, apposite for carrying out the idea giving rise to this chapter, may be offered.

Where a man executes a bond as surety for the principal obligor, he will be freed from liability on the bond by conduct of the obligee which is not consistent with good faith or fair and proper dealing, though perhaps scarcely amounting to what would popularly be termed fraud. Should the arrangement between the principal and obligee which induced the undertaking of the surety be altered in any material particular by the immediate parties to it, without notice to or assent, express or tacit, of the surety, he will be discharged. A bond was given by the obligor as surety, that a servant would, from time to time and at all times during the service, satisfactorily account for and pay over to his master all moneys received by the servant for the master's use. The servant made default in paying over moneys thus received, yet the master knowing—but not informing the surety—thereof, retained the servant in his service. It was held that in respect of any default subsequent to the retention the surety was discharged.[156]

The rule thus stated and applied is subject to some qualification: being meant for the benefit of the surety or contractor, it holds only where, if not applied, he would be prejudiced. If one man enters into a bond as surety for the performance by another of two things which are separate and distinct, a subsequent alteration of the principal's contract as to one of such things, without the knowledge and consent of the surety, would not operate to release the surety from his contract of suretyship as to the other of such things.[157] In such circumstances the surety is released *quoad* that undertaking in regard to which he would be prejudiced by the alteration made; in respect to the other undertaking he remains liable.

121. Where a check bearing a forged signature is inadvertently paid by the cashier of a bank, a question arises, on whom is the loss to fall? a query which must be answered on consideration of the nature of a check and the relation of a banker to his customer. Looking at a check when first drawn and held by the payee, the parties to it are drawer, payee, and banker, the nature of the contract between the first and second, and first and third, of these parties being as follows: The drawer undertakes to the payee that the draft shall be paid if presented at the bank during banking hours, at any date, subject to the operation of the statute of limitations, if not presented with six years from the time of its receipt (Art. 105). The nature of the undertaking of the banker towards his customer in relation to the check drawn upon him is to pay it, if presented within banking hours, and if there be in his (the banker's) hands sufficient funds of the customer standing to his credit, and applicable to the purpose of payment. Money deposited on current account with a banker is money lent to be repaid by the honoring of checks drawn by the customer upon the banker.[155] So

LEGAL PRINCIPLES APPLIED TO CONTRACTS. 137

that, as between banker and customer, a check paid by the banker *primâ facie* shows a return *pro tanto* of money previously deposited by the customer with him.

As the implied undertaking of the banker is to pay to the order of his customer, it is the banker's duty to become acquainted with his customer's handwriting, and therefore the banker who pays a forged check is in general liable to pay the amount again, *i. e.* he cannot debit his customer's account with the sum which has been thus paid. The banker, as the depositary of the customer's money, is bound to pay from time to time such sums as the customer may order. If unfortunately he pays money belonging to the customer upon an order which is not genuine, he (the banker) must suffer. The rule thus stated is subject to qualification. If it be the fault of the customer that the banker pays more than he ought, as where the amount specified in the check has been altered through gross negligence in the customer, the banker cannot be called on to pay again.

The rule, even thus qualified, which exposes to loss the banker who cashes a forged check might seem harsh did we not keep in view what was just now said, that the banker is bound to make himself acquainted with his customer's handwriting, and that where suspicion attaches to a check presented at his counter for payment, the banker may take a reasonable time for making inquiry before cashing the check.[139] A banker, moreover, has been protected against forgery by various statutory provisions.[160]

Although the forgery of a check is of comparatively rare occurrence, the subjoined additional instance, showing who must bear the loss ensuing from it, is given.

A check is essentially a negotiable and transferable instrument; it is, for instance, paid by a customer resident and banking in London to the tradesman with whom he deals; by that tradesman it is passed as cash to a country tradesman, who pays it in to his account at a country bank, by whom it is transmitted to their town agent, and by that establishment passed through the clearing-house to the bank upon which it was drawn; and thus the check, having operated in payment of a debt, comes back again to the party who drew it, the contract by him with the payee and the undertaking of the banker towards himself having been punctually performed. A check, we know, if drawn to bearer, passes by delivery; if drawn to order, by indorsement. Let us, then, suppose this state of facts: On payment of a sum of money by A. to B. & Co., bankers, a letter of credit is handed over by the bank in favor of C.; this letter of credit, bearing a forged indorsement, is afterwards presented to and paid by a country agent of the bank. Who is to suffer the loss? Upon these facts we may reply: "This is the ordinary case of bankers paying money upon a forged check. The bank has paid upon the forged signature of C., and that is no payment at all; therefore things are in the same situation as if the money were yet in the till of the bankers." [161]

122. A person about to insure his life may be cautioned as to one particular. In such a transaction the certainty of its due performance at the prescribed time is all-important; wherefore the contract under notice should, as regards the interests of the proposed insurer and his family, be in its inception wholly unimpeachable. Now, although a contract, as already shown (Arts. 48, 113) is liable to be vitiated by fraud, yet proof of fraud, of *mala fides* and the *scienter* being often difficult, it may be expedient, and has been found so, for an insurance company to introduce into a life policy, or to lay as the foundation of it some sort of warranty or undertaking, a non-compliance with which shall invalidate the policy; and where this practice is adopted, the person wishing to insure must be on

his guard. Very critical may otherwise be the position of those afterwards seeking to enforce the policy.

Let us suppose that A. enters into negotiations with an insurance company, with a view to effecting an insurance on his life, the practice of the office being, as just stated, to submit to the party proposing to insure a document containing the usual questions as to age, habits, and so forth, with a declaration to be subscribed by the person wishing to be insured, that the answers to such questions are correct and true throughout, and that if any fraudulent concealment or designedly untrue statement be contained therein, the premiums paid for the insurance shall be forfeited, and the policy shall be null and void—such declaration to be the basis of the contract between the insurers and insured. Suppose, further, that incorrect answers are given to sundry of the questions thus proposed to the insured, and that the insurance is effected; the insured dies, and a question thereupon arises between his representatives and the insurance company, whether the sum secured by the policy can be recovered. In such a case as this the policy might probably be admitted by the defendants, and the jury would have to decide as to the presence or absence of a fraudulent intent at the time when the answers were given by the deceased to the preliminary questions. The jury, we will assume, find that the answers were not designedly untrue; a question of law might upon that finding arise of this kind: Would a mere incorrect, not being a designedly false, statement in answer to a question proposed by the company, antecedently to executing the policy, vitiate it? For resolving this question, the court would, in the first place, regard the whole tenor of the policy and declaration upon which it was based, endeavoring to extract and gather from them the intention and meaning of the parties. Here certain rules of construction might fairly be applied; the language of a policy of insurance is prepared by the company which grants it, therefore the language used in it must be construed in that sense which a prudent person about to insure, looking at it, would have assigned to it. Should an ambiguous phrase occur in such a document—a phrase so worded perhaps that it might be understood in one sense, whilst it was really framed and proffered in another—the rule of construction requires that such phrase shall be taken in a sense adverse to the party using it (Art. 115, *ad fin.*) The result of such reasoning might well be that a policy so worded as supposed would be held good and binding as against the company, albeit some incorrect answers had been given to the questions proposed by the company prior to its execution.¹⁶²

A policy of life insurance contained a proviso that "if the declaration which serves as the basis of the insurance is not in every respect true, the insurance shall be void." The answers to the questions put on the part of the company to the party proposing to insure were declared to be truly set forth, nevertheless, the fact that one material particular thus deposed to was untrue, though not so to the knowledge of deponent, was held to have avoided the policy.¹⁶³

There is no necessary discrepancy between the decisions cited. In any such case the language of the policy must be looked at to show what was in the mind of those who made it. The object of the proviso was to protect the company against incorrect representations, irrespective of the question, to them immaterial, whether the misstatements were made *scienter* and fraudulently or not. If, moreover, A., relying on B.'s statement or representation, chooses to guarantee as a fact that which B. as affirmed to him to be such, A. does this at his own risk and peril, and must abide the consequences if what B. has stated proves to be untrue. Responsibilities for the acts and defaults of others are constantly underaken in commercial transactions. A merchant sells a cargo of goods which he warrants to be of a given quality, not because he has seen or personally knows anything about the goods, but merely because he bought them with a warranty. Another merchant contracts to deliver goods on a given day, trusting to the engagement of the person from whom he bought that the vendor will deliver on that day. It is one of the necessities of commerce that men should act upon the faith of each other's engagements.[164]

122. A state of things has already been adverted to (Art. 65) such as this: A. and B. contract together, and afterwards, without default by either party, performance of the contract with a view to effecting what the parties to it had contemplated becomes impossible, whereupon the questions arise: Does this affect, and if so how, their reciprocal rights and remedies? Of course express provision may be made in the contract for such a contingency. The charterer of a ship might agree to load with all possible dispatch a cargo of coals at a port named, "strike of pitmen excepted;" then, if a strike of probably long duration began, the charterer would be excused from putting the coals on board, and would have no right to call on the shipowner to wait till the strike was over. The ship-

owner would be excused from keeping his ship waiting, and would have no right to call on the charterer to load at a future time. The express exception in the case put operates as an excuse for him who was to do the particular act, and saves him from liability for breach of contract. It further enables the contractee, as it were, to retire from the contract.

Where an implied exception is insisted on, more difficulty may arise. A. enters the service of B., becomes ill and cannot perform his work. No action would lie against him for this non-feasance, and B., without waiting for A.'s recovery, might hire a fresh servant, provided that A.'s illness were such as to frustrate the object of the engagement of hiring in a business sense. So if A. engages B. to make a sketch of some passing event for an illustrated journal, and B. is attacked with blindness which will probably disable him for six months from following his vocation, A. could maintain no action for breach of contract against B., but he might procure some one else in lieu of B. to make the drawing. In such a case the exception is implied, and is deducible from the very nature of the contract.

Whether express or implied, an exception such as spoken of operates to release the contractee from his engagement, as well as to relieve the contractor. A., a shipowner, entered into a charter-party, by which the ship chartered was to proceed with all possible dispatch, " dangers and accidents of navigation excepted," from Liverpool to Newport, and there load a cargo of iron rails for San Francisco. The day after leaving Liverpool the ship got aground, and sustained injuries which could not be repaired till some eight months had elapsed. In the mean time the charterers threw up the charter-party and chartered another vessel for San Francisco; they were held justified in doing so. The vessel, owing to the mishap, was prevented from reaching Newport within a reasonable time, or in time for the adventure contemplated: the charterers, therefore, were discharged, though the shipowner was free from liability, inasmuch as the delay arose from an excepted peril.[165] By the decision thus given equal justice seems to have been done, and the principle on which it rests might readily be applied in other cases.

123. The legal rights of one who feels aggrieved by a supposed breach of contract may be ascertained by considering the proofs *pro* and *con.* which would be needed at Nisi Prius if he should go thither for redress, and these proofs may sometimes

be briefly enumerated without much resort to technicalities. For example, the undermentioned proofs must be forthcoming to support an action against a railway company for delay caused through the missing of a train by which the complainant had intended to take or continue his journey: The ticket issued to, and paid for by the passenger, the time-table or table of trains issued by authority of the company, and extrinsic facts which might show a contract or undertaking by the defendants.

The language of the ticket indicates simply that the defendants will convey the plaintiff from A. to B. by the specified line of railway, and the only relevant duty which the law raises out of the contract thus evidenced is that the passenger shall be carried in a reasonable time. Even this duty may be qualified by conditions inserted in the time-table, to which the ticket usually refers, though such conditions would not avail the company if the delay complained of were unreasonable or willful. The fact, indeed, of an inevitable accident having happened, or of some natural impediment having presented itself to the continuance of the traffic along a line of railway, might relieve the company from responsibility in respect of damage resulting from complainant's detention which otherwise would have attached to them.[166]

The train bill of a company such as spoken of might afford cogent evidence in support of the contract contended for by plaintiff. It usually, however, if not always, contains an express stipulation that the company do not guarantee the arrival and departure of trains at the times specified, so that the plaintiff might be put out of court on production of the time-table.

As to the last point, the only legitimate evidence other than the two items mentioned would be such as this: A statement by an authorized official of the company that the train in question would start, or would arrive at a particular time, or admissions made on behalf of the company in a correspondence with their manager or other accredited agent. Clearly, however, the mere talk of or expression of opinion by a porter or such like servant of the company would not suffice to raise a specific contract such as adverted to.[167]

So a plaintiff claiming compensation from a railway company for a personal hurt sustained by him whilst being conveyed on their line must give such evidence at Nisi Prius as that the jury may reasonably find, looking at the facts before them, that there had been " negligence " on the part of defendant, and no " contributory negligence " on the part of plaintiff—negligence being the want of that degree of care which a person of common sense might reasonably be expected to take under the circumstances, and contributory negligence disentitling the complainant to redress where by the exercise of ordinary care he might have avoided the consequences of defendants' negligence. Proof of negligence in this class of cases may consist in what was said by the company's servants when the accident occurred, or in their conduct or in that of the complainant. What a railway porter says in such a case, acting in the regular course of his employment, may well bind the company, though the true meaning of what he says may need to be carefully considered. Is the announcement of the name of a station, coincident with the stoppage of a train thereat, to be taken as an invitation to passengers to alight? If the train goes beyond the platform, so that it might be dangerous to alight from it, was sufficient notice of the danger, and that the train would back, given by the servants of the company? Was the plaintiff in fault in attempting to get out when the train had passed the platform?[168]

In like manner, where plaintiff sues a railway company for bodily hurt done him through their negligence (Chap. VI) whilst passing along a highway crossed by the line of railway, a very nice question for the judge at Nisi Prius may be: Is there any evidence for the jury of negligence by the defendants? If not, the verdict must be for them, or there must be a nonsuit. Much may here depend on the credibility of the company's servants, called on their behalf to show that, when the accident occurred, the usual precautions for warning and protecting the public had been taken.[169]

By looking at the contract between a railway company and a passenger on their line, and considering the duty of a carrier towards his passenger at common law, *i. e.*, irrespective of express contract or of statutory provisions, we must measure the liability of the former towards the latter. At common law, the obligation imposed on the carrier towards a passenger is to take all due care—the utmost care —to prevent any accident happening to him whilst *in transitu*. If, however, there be evidence showing that the passenger has himself been guilty of some wrong or illegal conduct with reference to the carrier, as, by entering a railway carriage without a ticket and with intent to defraud the company, or by misconducting himself when there, such illegal act, the wrongful intrusion or misconduct, might disentitle the passenger to redress.[170] The liability of a railway company, even for gross negligence causing bodily hurt, may be put aside by a notice worded to that effect, and incorporated with the contract between the traveler and the company. A railway company, for instance, undertakes to carry gratuitously a drover in charge of cattle in a truck, but declines liability for negligence. It is competent to the company to do so, and they will not in this case incur responsibility, even if the negligence be gross, the contract being subject to a condition exempting them therefrom.[171]

Besides the care which a railway company is bound to take of a passenger whilst actually *in transitu*, the company ought, by proper precautions, to prevent, so far as may be, the happening of any accident at a station, either by the undue crowding of the public to the trains, or by persons crossing the line at a dangerous moment, or otherwise. They should, therefore, have directions for the guidance of passengers to the trains, or from one part of a station to another, legibly posted up, and the stations should be sufficiently lighted for the safety and protection of strangers. Such an obligation is laid on a railway company in virtue of a general principle of law, that a person who invites another to come on his premises, must be deemed to have undertaken with regard to that person a duty to take reasonable care that the premises on which he invites him to come—the approach to the premises as well as the exit therefrom—shall be in such a state as not to expose the person using them in consequence of the invitation to undue or unreasonable danger. Such is the implied engagement of a railway company to any ordinary passenger who comes on their premises. It is part of their contract with him. Not unfrequently, however, a person—a drover, perhaps, in charge of cattle—is carried *gratis* by the company, and under a condition that he travels at his own risk, and when this is so, the company are exempted from liability for that which would have been negligence as against an ordinary passenger. They expressly claim to be free from liability for the default of their servants, and from the consequences of incidental risks, both before and after the actual *transitus*, arising from the state of their premises.[172]

Duties owing towards a railway company by a traveler taking goods with him by train are set forth or indicated in the by-laws of the company, which have been officially approved and sanctioned, and are binding on customers of the company. Any act done in fraud or breach of such a by-law may be summarily punishable, or may avail to relieve the company from responsibility for the loss of the goods. Let us suppose that a railway company, on whose line the plaintiff was a passenger, had publicly announced that they would not take merchandise as passengers' luggage, but that, if a passenger took merchandise with him, he was to pay at a certain rate for its carriage. Let us further suppose that this rule of the company was known to the plaintiff, but, nevertheless, that he took with him into the carriage a case containing merchandise, not stating to the company what he did. Under such circumstances the company would not be liable for its loss, for the plaintiff, in breach of the by-laws, intended to have the goods conveyed in the carriage with him, and thus to escape the obligation of paying for their conveyance as merchandise. Upon the facts put, there could not exist, in law or in reason, any contract between the plaintiff and the company touching those goods, upon the breach or in default of the performance of which the plaintiff could have a right enforceable against the company.[173]

Fair and honest dealing should, of course, be observed by every man towards another with whom he may be brought into privity. Fraud, such as exemplified, will nullify a *primâ facie* contract, and reduce to nothing the duty which might be thought to flow from it.

CHAPTER VI.

A TORT—WHAT IT IS.

"Il ne faut pas être étonné trouver dans les lois . . tant de règles, de restrictions, d'extensions, qui multiplient les cas particuliers, et semblent faire un art de la raison même."—MONTESQUIEU.

"If men will multiply injuries, actions must be multiplied too."—LORD HOLT.

124. A "TORT" is a wrong done by one person to another, the term being used in civil, not in criminal procedure; and the law set forth in the following pages is of great and increasing importance, because injuries new in kind are almost daily presenting themselves, and wrongs long recognized as such are becoming more frequent and more hurtful.

The mere infringement or invasion of a right constitutes in general injury for which an action will lie. Such an injury may be constituted by an assault, by false imprisonment, by bodily hurt done through carelessness, and so forth. If A. unlawfully place a part of his foot on B.'s land, this is in law a trespass. If a man fails to keep his cattle on his own land, so that they get into his neighbor's field, it is *primâ facie* a trespass. The act of the animals in voluntarily going on to another person's land would be as much a trespass as if they had been driven thither by their owner. In general our law does not concern itself with very trifling matters, but a trespass to land infringing the right to its exclusive occupancy is actionable.

125. A tort to land or realty may in its nature be indirect; it may be constituted by a wrongful act producing damage. For instance, A. so unskilfully manages his vessel that by the force of the wind or tide it is driven against and damages the pier or jetty of B.; A. is liable for the consequence of his negligence.[174] And although A. would not in general be liable for damage resulting from inevitable accident, sometimes an exception to this rule occurs in virtue of express enactment, the owner of a vessel having by force of statutory words been held liable to make good the amount of damage done to the works of a certain harbor board caused by inevitable accident from stress of weather.[175]

126. The nature of torts or wrongs done to personal or chattel property may be thus exemplified: The finder of a jewel has a better title to it than any other person save its absolute and rightful owner, and by reason of such special property in it, may sue one who gets hold of the jewel and detains

it from him.[176] If a pledgee deals with the pledge in a manner inconsistent with his contract, and other than is allowed by law for the payment of his debt, as by disposing of the reversionary interest of the pledgor in it; and if the pledgee thus causes the pledgor difficulty in re-obtaining possession of the pledge on payment of the sum due upon it, and so does him damage, the pledgee commits an actionable wrong against the pledgor.[177] If a horse be let on hire to A., and be killed by the violent driving of B., a stranger, an action of trespass will lie at suit of A., the party hiring and in actual possession of the horse, against B., whilst C., its owner, might sue B. for the damage done to his (A.'s) reversionary interest or property in the horse.[178] A. gratuitously allows B. to ride his horse, which, whilst used by B., sustains hurt through C.'s negligence; an action might be brought by the owner of the horse against C., because, in contemplation of law, the mere gratuitous permission to use the horse would not take it out of the possession of the owner; his possession would, under the circumstances supposed, be constructive.[179]

To support an action for wrongfully detaining goods, it will be for plaintiff to show his right to the immediate or present possession of them: *ex. gr.*, the purchaser of goods kept by the vendor as subject to his lien for unpaid purchase money could not sue a wrong-doer for the goods, having obviously no right to the immediate possession of them,[180] and therefore not being the proper person to complain of the wrongful withholding of the goods, and to seek compensation for the wrong.

127. The infringement of a right differing altogether from that to tangible property—for instance, the interest of an author in a literary work, of an inventor in a patent, of a manufacturer in a trademark, of an upholsterer in a registered design— might clearly be actionable, and might constitute a grievous wrong. So the malicious rejection of a vote by the official appointed to receive it might be the ground of an action in which perplexing questions as to the franchise, and as to the mode in which the officer should exercise his functions, might arise.[181] Very recently, in an action for an assault, a defense was set up justifying it, founded on the statute 35 & 36 Vict. c. 33, s. 9, the question involved being whether a candidate at a parliamentary or municipal election has a general right to be present in a polling station during the election, or whether he has merely a qualified right to be present for a specific purpose, that, *viz.*, of undertaking the duties of an agent or of assisting his appointed agent. The question thus raised was

decided in favor of the plaintiff, his right to be present generally, and not merely for a specific purpose, being thus established.[182] From any such case we may infer that a damage is not necessarily pecuniary, but that "an injury imports a damage when a man is thereby hindered of his right."[158]

128. The words of Lord Holt above cited are justly celebrated, and on the occasion of uttering them the same illustrious man enunciated another proposition—that where a new act of Parliament is made for the benefit of "the subject, if a man be hindered from the enjoyment of it, he shall have an action against the person who obstructed him." In applying this rule we must, however, discriminate between the case where an absolute right is thus conferred, as the right to vote at an election, and the case where a duty is imposed on one towards others, and a right of action is thus impliedly given for breach of such duty. In the former case real substantial damage need not be shown to have accrued to the complainant; in the latter it must. When a duty, to be performed gratuitously, has been imposed on a company by statute, and the company have consented that it should be put on them in consideration of benefits conferred on them by the act, a correlative right, enforceable against the company, becomes vested in some one should

the duty be violated to his damage.[154] If the duty of keeping towing paths and river banks in repair be imposed upon a body incorporated and regulated by statute, and they neglect to perform that duty, a person who has sustained a particular damage from such neglect, not common to the public at large, may bring his action to recover pecuniary compensation for the damage which he has thus sustained. Here the remedy specified becomes available when a breach of duty having been committed, damage has resulted from it. If such a body corporate keep open a towing path and take toll for its use, they are under an obligation to those whom they invite to use it, either to take reasonable care that they be not, in doing so, exposed to undue danger, or to warn them duly against such danger.[155]

129. A tort or wrong such as has been thus far glanced at is apparently simple in its nature, although doubtless in discussions concerning it points of difficulty may occur. Facts, however, present themselves to the observer, out of which a right of action more complex in its character may originate, founded perhaps on breach of duty, on negligence, malice, or fraud producing damage, or on express enactment. The following articles and paragraphs have been framed to elucidate this subject by reference to facts, taken almost indifferently,

likely to arise, and by a suggestion of the law applicable to them.

The phrase "breach of duty," just used, is of very wide significance, and may include the several ingredients of "negligence," "malice," and "fraud;" it may also be exemplified by reference to reciprocal duties and obligations, a breach of which does not necessarily involve any one of the ingredients mentioned. A breach of duty may consist in malfeasance or non-feasance, *i. e.*, in wrongful commission or omission.

130. A duty may exist, may be imposed, on a person, in virtue of vicinage.

In mineral districts the surface of land often belongs to one proprietor, whilst the strata underlying it belong to another, and when this is so, the owner of the coal or minerals must so work his strata as to leave sufficient support for the soil above, and so as not to prejudice the enjoyment of it. The right in regard to the working of the mine or colliery may, however, be regulated or amplified by express contract, or by implication arising out of it, or by local custom.[186]

The owner of a coal mine on a level higher than that of his neighbor worked out his coal, leaving no barrier between his mine and the mine on the lower level, so that water penetrating and percolating through the boundaries of the lower mine flowed into it and obstructed its owner in getting his coal. It was held that the owner of the lower mine had no ground of complaint as against the owner of the upper mine, for this latter proprietor had a right to mine and remove all his coal. The damage sustained by the plaintiff was caused by the natural flow or percolation of water from the upper strata. There was no obligation on the defendant to protect the plaintiff against the water. It was for the plaintiff to erect or leave a sufficient barrier to keep out the water, or to adopt means for so conducting the water that it should not impede him in his workings. The water was, under the circumstances stated, merely left by the defendant to flow in its natural course; no legal duty was violated by him; the loss sustained was not caused by his default.[187]

Let us suppose, again, that there are owners of two adjacent mines, of which one is on a higher level than the other, and that the defendant, owner of the upper mine, has not merely suffered water to flow through his mine without leaving a barrier between it and the mine below, but that, in order to work his own mine beneficially, he has pumped up water which has afterwards passed into the plaintiff's mine, in addition to that which would have naturally reached it, and so caused him damage.

This will be actionable, though done by defendant without negligence, and with a view merely to the working of his own mine. The reason being that in the performance of the defendant's act the plaintiff was damaged; and whether that act were skillfully or unskillfully performed would be immaterial as regards the right of action.[188] There is disclosed upon the facts put a breach of duty owing by defendant to his neighbor. The ingredients in the tort are breach of duty and damage thence resulting.

131. A landowner who collects on his land in unusual quantities anything, *ex. gr.*, water, likely to do mischief if it escapes, is *primâ facie* bound to prevent it from escaping, and is answerable for damage consequent on its escape. Where this proposition applies, a remedy by action will be available for him whose land has been invaded or whose movable property has been destroyed by the escaping element. Here a duty owing to any one in the vicinage has been disregarded by defendant, whose liability results from his breach of such duty, and is not grounded on the idea that he has been guilty of negligence. Should there, under circumstances seemingly like those imagined, be no duty owing by defendant to his neighbor, and no negligence be apparent in his conduct, the proposi-

tion stated would not apply, and great care may be needed in distinguishing between such states of facts.[189]

132. The owner of land or realty may sometimes be justified in protecting it, though in so doing he cause damage to his neighbor. Here, again, the test applicable is this—Was any duty imposed on the alleged wrong-doer towards the complainant to abstain from doing what he did, whether in virtue of vicinage or otherwise? If there were no such duty imposed, no breach of duty could have been committed, and the foundation of a right of action to recover compensation for damage caused would wholly fail. A flood, for instance, is a common enemy, against which every man has a right to defend himself, and a man is not bound to stand by and see his property destroyed, out of fear lest, in protecting it, he may cause injury to his neighbor. The law allows a kind of reasonable selfishness on such an occasion. There may be a conflict between duties, between that which a man owes to himself and his dependents and that which he owes to his neighbor; and the greater or more imperative of these duties must prevail.[190] True it is that a man should in general so use his own property as not to damage his neighbor or his neigh-

bor's property. This rule, however, must be qualified in the manner stated.

In general, moreover, a person having the exclusive use of water running on to his land, may reasonably enjoy it in such manner as he likes, and apply it to some novel purpose more beneficial to himself than previously, although a riparian owner higher up the stream, having wrongfully diverted it, might complain that his rights had thus been abridged, inasmuch as for the wrongful act of diversion heavier damages might have to be paid by him than before. It is the necessary effect of every appropriation of running water to a new and more beneficial use, that a wrongful diversion or abstraction of it entails a larger measure of liability.[191] The argument thus urged against the exercise by plaintiff of his right was somewhat artificial, and was held untenable, regard being had to recognized principles of law.

133. It may be well here to observe that Parliament, when called on to legislate respecting public works, necessarily allows that to be done which may for a time prejudice the public or individuals; usually, however, it prescribes the mode of doing it, and enjoins what shall be done to mitigate or compensate for the annoyance caused. And even when this is otherwise, our common law may raise out of

the words of an enactment a duty pertinent to the occasion, although not expressly stated or defined therein. For instance, where persons are authorized by statute to create what would *prima facie* amount to an indictable nuisance, as impeding the traffic along a highway, they are bound, without any express clause being inserted in the act, to put and keep up for the public a proper substitute for the old way, such as a bridge. If a railway company is empowered to lay rails at a level crossing, and accordingly lays such rails as may be necessary for the traffic, the rails must be laid down and kept so as to cause as little injury or danger to the public as possible.[192] In such a case the particular duty is imposed by statute, and an action for breach or nonobservance of it causing damage will lie at suit of the injured person.

134. It must have become obvious from several of the preceding articles (see particularly Arts. 12, 126, 130) that a distinction is to be noticed between absolute and qualified rights—between that which is mine exclusive of any right in another or in others, present or future, and that of which I have but a qualified possession, a possession subservient to the contemporary or future use of the property by third persons.

Reverting to a state of things supposed in Art.

12. If I place a log of wood across a public path, and injury be thereby caused to a passer-by, the soil being my own, but the public or individuals having a right of way over it, an action will lie against me, because there is a privilege vested in others of going along the path without interruption. If, however, there be no right of way over it, I may place any obstruction on my own land, and a stranger who has no right to be there, and sustains damage consequent on his own trespass, cannot sue me successfully for the damage so sustained. A., seized in fee of waste land adjoining a highway, digs a pit in the waste, distant a dozen yards or so from the highway, and B.'s horse, escaping into the waste, falls into the pit. B. cannot sue A. for damage thence accruing, for A. sunk the pit on his own land, and B. was to blame for allowing his horse to escape into the waste. Here of course we must suppose that no duty to maintain or repair fences was imposed on A., for if such a duty were imposed, and B.'s horse had strayed through a gap in the fence on to A.'s land, the result at law would have been different.[193] Facts analogous to those put are frequently brought before a jury in actions against railway companies. Sometimes the claim for damages resulting from a breach of duty such as indicated is founded on the

unwritten or customary, sometimes on the statute law.

135. A duty akin to such as last treated of may be owing to the public generally, or to some individual who has been brought into relation with him on whom it is laid, or who has in some way assumed and undertaken it.

The owner or person in possession of premises adjoining a highway, will be liable for a nuisance to such highway if he allow on his premises, an unprotected excavation so near the road that a person lawfully using it, and exercising ordinary caution, by accidentally slipping, might fall into the hole. And, generally speaking, the responsibility for such a nuisance rests on him who is in occupation of the premises whereon the nuisance complained of exists. It may be that other persons are also liable, but the occupier, who probably knows most about it, is bound to see that there is no dangerous nuisance upon the premises, and should he allow one to exist there, he is guilty of a breach of duty whence, if damage result to an individual, the owner or occupier may incur civil liability.[194] A peculiarity may here be noticed; the excavation being within the boundary of A.'s (the owner's or occupier's) premises, B., the injured person, is technically a trespasser in the eye of the law, in transgressing the line of demarcation between the highway and A.'s private premises, and yet may recover damages from A. in respect of the hurt sustained by him through falling into the hole; the reason of this being that a public nuisance has been created or permitted within the boundary of A.'s land, causing damage.[195]

From what was stated in Arts. 13 and 156, we may deduce that where a person resorts to premises in the course of business, on the express or implied invitation of their occupier, such person himself using reasonable care is entitled to expect the occupier to use like care to prevent damage from any cause of unusual danger, which he knows or ought to know of, existing on the premises. Where there is evidence of neglect, that is for the jury. If there be evidence that the plaintiff was on the defendant's premises on business by his, the defendant's, express or tacit invitation—that there was an unusual source of danger existing there known to or within the knowledge of the defendant, and that damage occurred to the plaintiff by reason of the defendant or his servants not using sufficient means to avert and warn the plaintiff of it, the defendant will be liable as for breach of duty causing damage.[196]

Cases such as the above, in which of course the

facts may infinitely vary, have interest for the legal analyst, as showing and rendering quite appreciable the distinction between breach of duty and negligence.

136. Bodily hurt is sometimes caused by the attack of an animal, domesticated or not. A mishap of this kind is frequently occurring, and is peculiar as regards the law applicable to it and the proofs requisite *pro* and *con.* at Nisi Prius, when an action originates out of it. The owner of a domesticated or other animal not naturally inclined to mischief— for example, a dog—is not liable for bodily hurt done by it, unless it can be shown that such owner previously had notice of the animal's mischievous propensity, or unless the damage done was attributable to neglect on his part; it is in general necessary in an action for injury done by such an animal to allege and prove the *scienter*. Proof of the *scienter* may be by showing the fact of actual damage having been done by the animal on a previous occasion, to the defendant's knowledge, which may be evidenced by his presence at the time when the mischief was done, or by notice to him of the fact.

Notice may be either to the defendant directly or indirectly to him—as through his wife or servant —and though notice to a servant or to a wife might not necessarily suffice to fix the defendant in such a case with liability, yet should some additional fact be established—as that the wife had assisted in carrying on her husband's business, and that a formal complaint had been made to the wife when on her husband's premises, and for the purpose of being communicated to him—these proofs taken together might well suffice to fortify the plaintiff's case, though the main question involved, as one of fact, would be for the jury. If the owner of a dog puts it under the care of a servant, the servant's knowledge of the dog's ferocity is deemed to be the knowledge of the master.[197]

The owner of an animal undomesticated is bound to keep it in sure custody, and will be liable, should it escape and injure any one, to pay him compensatory damages.[198] Here specific proof of negligence would not be needed, and the *scienter* would be presumed.

In either of the cases just put, the rule of law must be stated and explained to the jury by the judge, and in any case such as first mentioned difficulty may be felt as to whether the proofs of the *scienter* adduced suffice to fix the defendant with liability.

137. Negligence is fruitful in producing damage; an act done negligently having been done otherwise than it would have been by a reasonable man

guided by considerations such as ordinarily regulate the conduct of human affairs. Negligence may also consist in the omitting to do something which a reasonable man would do.

Negligence causing damage may lay the foundation of an action, and although something more than a mere *scintilla* of proof of negligence would be needed in support of the plaintiff's case, the bare facts established in evidence may be such as to show that the defendant was negligent. *Ex. gr.*, suppose that A., walking in a public street, past B.'s warehouse, is injured by a bale of goods falling from an upper flooring of it upon him, there would, upon proof of these facts at Nisi Prius, be *primâ facie* evidence of negligence as against B., which he, to entitle himself to a verdict, ought to rebut.

138. Difficulty as to the proof of negligence and its sufficiency often arises; well-trained, experienced lawyers differing in regard to it, and the mere fact of protracted litigation thus ensuing, guided and directed by eminent practitioners, suffice to show, not the uncertainty of our law, for its principles relevant and applicable to the facts *sub judice* have been clearly determined, but the perplexities which may have to be encountered where fact and law are blended together, and where consequently the

judges may eventually be called on to perform in some sort the functions of jurymen.[199]

Notwithstanding the difficulty adverted to, the judge at Nisi Prius will, in a case such as supposed, have to say whether there is or is not such *quantum* of evidence as to justify him in submitting it to the jury, and the due performance of this part of his duty may involve perplexing considerations. Proofs, indeed, are sometimes so much in conflict, or so nicely balanced, that in the same case similarly presented, by different juries different verdicts will be given, and the presiding judge will sometimes acknowledge himself at fault in determining on which side is the preponderance of evidence.

139. To the matter now before us some brief reference has already been made (Art. 123), and a rule has been stated of this kind: Where the damage complained of was caused entirely by defendant's negligence, the plaintiff would be entitled to recover. If the plaintiff himself so far contributed to the mishap by his own negligence or want of ordinary care and caution, that but for such negligence or want of care the misfortune would not have happened, the plaintiff will be precluded from redress. Mere negligence or want of ordinary care or caution would not, however, disentitle him to recover if the defendant might, by the exercise of

care on his part, have avoided the consequences of the neglect or carelessness of plaintiff.[200] It may readily be supposed that, in applying to facts about which the proofs are usually conflicting, a rule so critically worded, mistakes are often made, and accordingly many cases are to be found in the reports which have been discussed *in banc*, involving the doctrine of contributory negligence.

This doctrine has been held applicable under circumstances to which, at first sight, it might not have been thought so. The parent of a child of very tender years may, by contributory negligence, disentitle the child hurt through the defendant's default from obtaining redress in damages—the child being so far identified with the parent, that an action brought in the child's name would not be maintainable.[201] A servant, whilst doing his master's work, becomes for some purposes identified with him; he could not, for instance, recover against defendant for damages caused by negligence or breach of duty, where the master himself, by reason of his neglect to do what he ought to have done, would have been precluded from recovering.[202] A passenger by an omnibus is so far identified with the driver that the negligence of the latter, contributing to a collision with another omnibus, may disentitle the passenger to redress as against its owner.[203] This same principle has been applied so as to identify, under analogous circumstances, a passenger by railway train with the engine-driver. At all events the question has been judicially suggested as worthy of consideration, whether, in a case of railway collision, with evidence of contributory negligence, a passenger sustaining bodily hurt therefrom could maintain an action for breach of contract against the company which carried him, and another action for negligence against the company whose servants caused the accident.[204]

140. Discussions respecting negligence have frequently arisen in actions brought under the remarkable statute known as Lord Campbell's act (9 and 10 Vict. c. 93, amended by 27 and 28 Vict. c. 95), which innovates on two established rules of our customary law—(1) that an action for bodily hurt cannot be maintained after the death of the injured person for the benefit of his estate; and (2) that where an act is in its nature felonious, the civil remedy, if any, in respect of it is merged, or rather suspended, until public justice shall have been satisfied by the prosecution of the offender. Lord Campbell's act provides that an action shall be maintainable by an executor or administrator for the benefit of certain of the surviving relatives of one whose death has been caused by a wrongful

act or by neglect or default, which, if death had not ensued, would have been actionable; and this statute further enacts, that for the negligent or wrongful act ending in death, compensation in damages may be enforced, although the death were caused under such circumstances as amount in law to felony.

141. It may naturally be asked how, where an action is successfully brought under the act referred to, the measure of damages ought to be determined? What considerations may influence the jury in assessing them? What description of evidence is to be deemed relevant for assessing them? To such queries these general answers must suffice: That where death is caused by negligence the jury are to give compensatory damages only—not vindictive or exemplary damages; further, that the jury are to exclude from their consideration as well the loss or suffering of the deceased himself as the mental anguish caused to his family by his death; that they should restrict themselves solely to estimating the damage resulting to the family therefrom; by reason of expenses to which they may have been thus put; by reason of the loss of salary (if any) enjoyed by the deceased, and benefiting his family; by reason of the loss of the profits of his business.

Such are the ordinary elements and considerations available for an assessment of damages under the statute mentioned. In an action brought under its provisions, the evidence of experts, such as accountants and actuaries, is admissible, and will sometimes remove difficulties which might be insurmountable by a jury thus unaided. Doubtless extraordinary facts may be suggested or imported into almost any given case which would render a satisfactory decision touching the amount of damages to be awarded extremely difficult. It seems, however, that mere remote contingencies could not be taken into account at all in the assessment of damages. To railway companies there can be no doubt that hardship has been caused through the readiness of juries to compensate individuals inordinately at their expense for damage sustained in consequence of the death of a relative through negligence.

142. In an action against a railway company, such as referred to, fraud by the complainant is very common, though proof of malpractice by him in connection with the claim advanced would materially jeopardize his case. Indeed, the conduct of the party to a suit may be of the highest importance in determining whether the cause of the action in which he is plaintiff, or the ground of defense if

he is defendant, is an honest and just one. If, for example, it be proved that a man suing in a court of justice has been suborning false testimony, and has tried to have recourse to perjury, it is strong to show that he knew that his cause of action was unrighteous; this is therefore evidence for the jury, not necessarily conclusive, but to be weighed by them in conjunction with other facts.

In an action by husband and wife for a personal hurt caused to the latter by the defendants' negligence, witnesses were called for the defense, who proved that the husband and a clerk in the office of the plaintiffs' attorney had jointly requested them (the witnesses) to give evidence in support of the plaintiffs' case, although plaintiffs knew that the persons thus applied to had not been present at the time when the accident happened. Such evidence was held to be receivable, as amounting to an admission by conduct that the plaintiffs' case was not good and genuine.[205]

Such a principle as stated may be applicable to the conduct of plaintiffs suing under Lord Campbell's act (9 & 10 Vict. c. 93), and seeking by false and fraudulent testimony to inflame the damages.

143. An attempt has been made—though happily it was unsuccessful—to extend quite unduly

the operation of Lord Campbell's act, by putting upon its provisions a construction of this kind. It was said that the statute gives to the personal representatives of the deceased, whose death has been caused by negligence, a right of action beyond that which the deceased himself would have had if he had survived, and based upon a different principle. It was contended that if bodily hurt were sustained by a person, and damages were recovered in respect of it by him, and his death afterwards resulted from that hurt, another action at suit of the personal representatives would lie to recover damages in respect of the injury and death. Similarly, it was urged, that if the claim of the deceased for the hurt sustained by him were compensated by a payment of money made to and accepted by him living, such payment or accord and satisfaction would not operate in bar of an action by his personal representatives, founded upon the above-mentioned act, to enforce additional compensation. The words of the statute, however, are not to be so strained, and all such contentions as referred to have, we may suppose, been set at rest.[206]

The point thus adjudged was one of much practical importance, it being customary for a railway company, so liable to be brought within the reach of Lord Campbell's act, to arrange with persons who have sustained bodily hurt through the negligence of their servants, the amounts of compensation to be paid them, and it would be hard indeed if, on the death of any one of the injured persons so compensated, in consequence of his injuries, another action grounded on the same transaction could be brought, with a successful issue, against the company.

144. Where an action is brought against a railway company to recover compensation for damage done to cattle which, through alleged non-feasance of the company, have got on to the line, questions difficult of solution may present themselves. Is the company liable at all for the act or non-feasance of its servants? If so, to whom? Was the duty, for breach of which the action is brought, owing to all persons alike, or is it owing to some section only of the community? and is the individual who seeks redress included in such section? A railway company is bound by statute (8 & 9 Vict. c. 20, s. 68) to maintain sufficient fences for the protection of the cattle of "the owners or occupiers" of land adjoining their line. This provision is for the benefit of all persons lawfully using the adjoining land; so that if a horse be on adjoining land, by license of the owner, and thence escape on to the line through a defective fence, which the company

ought to have repaired, and be killed by a passing train, the owner of the horse will be entitled to recover compensation by action from the company.[207]

145. Negligence, which as already stated, is one phase of breach of duty (Art. 129), may be evidenced in many ways, by reference to wholly dissimilar states of facts, to cases where and the parties who respectively complain of and are aggrieved by it, stand toward each other in different relations.

146. The inland trade of this country is very much carried on through the agency of commercial travelers, who make circuits through various districts, calling upon customers of firms which they represent, and extending, where possible, the dealings of their principals. Taking with them samples of goods often, though not bulky, of great value, and sojourning at inns, questions sometimes arise as to the liability of an innkeeper in respect of merchandise or luggage under such circumstances brought to his inn, and thence stolen or abstracted. What is the liability of the innkeeper in respect of a loss so sustained? For answering this question reference must be made generally to our customary law, as affected by express enactment.

The liability of an innkeeper, as custodian or bailee of property belonging to his guest, rested till the passing of a recent statute (26 & 27 Vict. c. 41) entirely on the common law, being set forth in a case decided *temp.* Lord Coke,[208] which shows that an innkeeper "is bound by day and night to keep safely the guest's goods and chattels," but, further, that the innkeeper "shall not be charged unless there be a default in him or his servants in the well and safe keeping and custody of their guests' goods and chattels within his inn."

By way of answer to a claim against the innkeeper, in respect of damage resulting from his alleged negligence or breach of duty, several grounds of defense may be available, a brief examination of which will further illustrate that part of the law concerning torts which is now under our notice.

(1) The innkeeper may show that the guest has himself been guilty of negligence conducing to the loss of his goods. A. whilst staying as a traveler at B.'s inn had stolen from him valuable property by a person who was afterward tried for and convicted of the theft. There was here some proof of negligence on the part of the plaintiff, and the rule of law applicable to the facts was thus stated: The goods remain under the charge of the innkeeper and the protection of the inn so as to make the innkeeper liable as for breach of duty, unless the negligence of the guest occasions the loss in such a

way as that the loss would not have happened if the guest had used the ordinary care that a prudent man may be reasonably expected to have taken under the circumstances.[209] Such an amount of negligence in the guest, as thus indicated, will accordingly excuse the innkeeper.

(2) Another sufficient ground of defense may be that the goods were retained by the guest in his own special care and custody. The plaintiff, a commercial traveler, went to the defendant's inn and was shown into the public room; he desired, however, to have and was allowed the use also of a private room in which to exhibit his goods for sale. The guest was told that he might lock the door of this room, but omitted to do so, and some of his goods were stolen. Upon these facts the innkeeper was held to be exonerated from liability. "If," it was judicially said, "there be evidence that the guest accepted the key, and took on himself the care of his goods, surely it is for the jury to determine whether the evidence of his receiving the key proves that he did it *animo custodiendi*, and with a purpose of exempting the innkeeper, or whether he took it merely because the landlord forced it on him, or for the sake of procuring greater privacy, in order to prevent persons from intruding themselves into his apartment."[210] And so in the case reported by

Lord Coke, and already cited, this hypothetical state of things is put, and the law in regard to it is stated: "The innkeeper requires his guest that he will put his goods in such a chamber, under lock and key, and then he will warrant them, otherwise not. The guest lets them lie in an outer court whence they are taken away: the innkeeper shall not be charged, for the fault is in the guest."

(3) The same old case affords a voucher for a third matter upon which the innkeeper may rely to relieve himself from liability when charged with negligence touching his guest's property, for in it we read that if the guest's servant, or he who comes or is lodged with him, steals or carries away his goods, the innkeeper shall not be charged, for there "the fault is in the guest to have such" a companion or servant.

(4) It would avail the innkeeper to show that the goods in question were lost or had perished through some inevitable casualty; and, in brief, the innkeeper cannot be charged as for negligence where loss arises from the complainant's own default, or from the act of God (Art. 78), or of the Queen's enemies;[211] nor shall he answer for anything that is out of his inn. So that if a man comes to a common inn, and delivers his horse to the ostler, and requires him to put the horse to pas-

ture, which is done, and the horse is stolen, the innkeeper shall not answer for it. On the other hand, although an innkeeper is *primâ facie* answerable for the safe keeping of a horse belonging to his guest which is put in the stable of the inn, yet should injury be done to it whilst in his custody, proof that the innkeeper has exercised due care in matter, and has properly attended to the horse, may be adduced in rebuttal of this liability, and to take away the plaintiff's cause of action.[212]

The liability of an innkeeper in respect of his guest's goods is now, by statute (26 & 27 Vict. c. 41), limited to £30, except in two cases. 1st. Where the goods have been stolen, lost or injured through the willful act, default, or neglect of the innkeeper or his servant; and, 2dly, where the goods have been deposited for safe custody with the innkeeper; who cannot, however, avail himself of this latter exception, should the deposit not have been made, by reason of his refusal to receive it, or his default.

147. A perusal of the foregoing article shows that the phrase "breach of duty" may be identical with the term "negligence." It is so under circumstances dissimilar from those just adverted to, and where, moreover, the relation of the complainant to

the person from whom redress is sought is altogether different.

Goods may be intrusted by their owner or bailed to another by contract or agreement, the stipulations wherein will, if sufficiently expressed, regulate the rights and liabilities of either party to it. If not sufficiently expressed, something may have to be implied by our customary law—for instance, an undertaking that a certain degree of care and diligence in regard to the subject-matter of the bailment shall be used—the law thus interposing, as it so often does, to complete what the parties themselves have left indefinite. A bailment induces important consequences at common law, without any express agreement between bailor and bailee directly pointing thereto. Thus, a bailee for hire not charged as a common carrier, is bound to use ordinary diligence, and to exercise reasonable skill in regard to, and in dealing with, the subject-matter of the bailment; he is irresponsible for any loss not occasioned by the ordinary negligence of himself or his servants. If such a bailee undertake "safely and securely" to carry, this will be understood as signifying that he will carry safely and securely with reference to the degree of care which under the circumstances the law requires of him, *i. e.*, that he will use such a reasonable degree of care that the customer shall incur no damage or loss through his (the carrier's) default. In a case like this our customary law is called on to adjust the obligations arising out of bailment, and it does so by reference to degrees of care and negligence which it is difficult adequately to characterize.

If the performance of his undertaking by the bailee be gratuitous, it obviously would not be reasonable to expect from him that degree of care and diligence which might fairly be required where he is to be remunerated for his trouble, and therefore proof that he has exercised even a slight degree of care and diligence may exonerate him from responsibility as bailee. But what are we to understand by slight diligence, or what by gross negligence? which, in legal phraseology, is said to exist where slight diligence is absent, and what are we to understand by reasonable care, an expression often met with in the perusal of cases about bailment.

Reasonable care and slight diligence would seem to be nearly equivalent expressions. At all events, where reasonable care had been taken of the chattel bailed, it could hardly be said that slight diligence was wanting, and the question what is reasonable care may have to be answered by reference to the nature, value, and quality of the thing bailed, and to the degree of skill which the bailee possesses or has professed himself able to exert. In the following chapter states of facts illustrating the nature of negligence, and the consequence of it as regards liability for damages, will be set forth.

Our customary law, then, making use of one or other of the expressions noticed, assumes to determine the liability of a bailee when not determined by contract, and, as regards certain species of bailments, the law has been announced long since, confirmed by authentic precedents, and handed down to us in a form which can readily be applied. As regards other species of bailments, peculiar and exceptional, the law has to be judicially declared on view of the facts which have occurred, so that a jury, from the proofs before them, may rightly determine not merely the existence or non-existence of negligence but, if existent, its degree—was its slight, gross, or culpable?

In performing this rather delicate duty, the jury will thus be aided by the judge, who might, for instance, have to explain to them that a person conveying goods may do so as a mere bailee *gratis*, or as a bailee for reward; may do so under an express contract; may do so as a common carrier by the customary law, or as a carrier within the scope of certain statutory provisions. Where in any case such as supposed there has been negligence, default, or misconduct on the part of the plaintiff, the task imposed on the jury may be onerous.

148. As social relations and mercantile transactions become more complex and involved, so are novel injuries committed, in respect of which, from time to time, new remedies must be devised. Resort will then be needed to first principles, and although on the one hand the law is strongly against the invention or creation of rights of action, on the other hand, where a wrong has actually been suffered by one person in consequence of the conduct of another, the maxim, *ubi jus ibi remedium* will, as far as possible, be upheld.[213] Within the reach of the maxim cited is the case where an untrue statement disparaging complainant's goods has been published without lawful occasion, and caused him special damage. In an action brought by one patentee of machinery against another, the following facts appeared in evidence: The plaintiff had been negotiating for the sale of his machines to different manufacturers, some of whom were already using the defendant's machines under licenses from him. The defendant wrote to these manufacturers stating that the plaintiff's machines infringed his patent, and that if used he would claim and enforce payment of royalties for their use, whereby the plaintiff

lost profits which would have accrued from the sale of his machines. It was adjudged on these facts that, malice being proved, the defendant would be liable, although such an action had never before been brought. An unfounded assertion that the owner of real property has not title to it, if made with malice express or implied, and if productive of special damage, is clearly actionable, and there is no reason why a similar proposition should not hold in regard to personalty.[214]

An unusual kind of tort directed against chattel property recently formed the ground of complaint, viz., that defendant maliciously and without reasonable or probable cause procured the plaintiff's ship to be arrested under a warrant from the county court, in which was pending an action against plaintiff for the price of necessaries supplied to his ship, whereby plaintiff lost the use of his ship, was deprived of the benefits which would thence have resulted, and was "much injured and damnified" in his credit and otherwise.[215]

149. A malicious act directed against a person's reputation may lead to more serious results than when leveled at his property, and will be more severely dealt with by a jury.

It is permissible for any man to prefer an indictment against another for an alleged crime, but when the indictment is disposed of in favor of the accused, an action will lie at his suit for damages against the prosecutor, provided proofs be forthcoming to show that the charge was false and malicious, and made without reasonable or probable cause.[216] Malice *per se* is not actionable, but malice causing damage often is so.

150. Malice is an essential ingredient in an action for defamation. As regards defamatory words, however, our law distinguishes between those which are written and published and those which are spoken, for the writing and publishing of such words indicates an intent to injure which may be absent when words are spoken. In either case the occasion may justify and privilege the act.

In an action for slander three primary questions may present themselves: 1st. Were the words actionable *per se?* 2dly. If not so, did damage to the complainant result from them, as a natural and reasonable consequence of speaking them? 3dly. Did the occasion privilege the defendant?[217] All disparaging words causing damage which flows naturally and immediately from them are actionable, and some communications are deemed to be of so hurtful a nature that our law presumes damage to result from them without actual proof of it.

Slander is actionable without proof of special

damage, if spoken of plaintiff with reference to his trade, and calculated to injure him therein.

In the class of cases secondly mentioned, *i. e.*, where the act complained of is not in itself necessarily injurious to complainant, but becomes so by reason of special damage caused by it, the special damage has been set forth and proved as the gist of the action, and in order to establish the injury.

In an action for libel, it is for the judge to determine upon the evidence whether the words complained of are reasonably capable of the defamatory meaning ascribed to them, and if they are not so, he will withdraw the case from the jury, and a nonsuit or a verdict for the defendant will ensue.[218]

At the trial of an action for defamation, written or verbal, it is for the judge to determine whether the occasion of writing or speaking criminatory language which would otherwise be actionable repels the inference of malice—constituting what is called a privileged communication—and if at the close of the plaintiff's case there is no proof of malice, intrinsic or extrinsic, it is for the judge to direct a nonsuit or a verdict for the defendant, without leaving the question of malice to the jury. A different course would, indeed, be contrary to principle, and would deprive the honest transactions of business and social intercourse of the protection due to them.[219]

In an action for slander, the fact that an apology for the slanderous imputation was offered before action brought is admissible in evidence in reduction of the damages; and in an action against the proprietor of a newspaper or other periodical for libel, the defendant may set up, by way of defense, that the libelous matter was inserted without actual malice and without gross neglect, and that before action brought he has inserted or offered to insert an apology for the libel in such paper or periodical, paying at the same time a sum of money into court as amends for the injury done to plaintiff.[220] If, instead of thus pleading in an action for libel, a defense of justification be set up, it may be taken into account by the jury in their assessment of damages, as showing express malice. The *animus* of defendant is thus deemed to be almost conclusively established, and heavy damages may be given.

In an action for defamation, ample compensation, so far as money can compensate for the injury inflicted, will usually be awarded to the aggrieved person, nor would the court, unless such damages were beyond all bounds and reason, interfere with the discretion of the jury thus exercised. For inadequacy of damages a new trial is seldom granted. It was so, however, recently, in an action for slander, the smallness of the amount awarded showing that the jury had made a compromise, and, instead of deciding the issues submitted to them, had agreed to find for the plaintiff with nominal damages.[221] In the case cited, the slanderous words imputed to plaintiff the commission of an indictable offense, and were calculated to be extremely injurious to his character. Hence, it could not be considered that any verdict had really been given— the very meaning of the word "verdict" having been falsified.

151. A wrongful act, more prevalent now than formerly, consists in fraud producing damage, and as fraud may be ground of defense to an action, so may it lay the foundation of one.

Instances of fraudulent misrepresentation have been already given (Arts. 14, 49, 80, 97), and are almost daily presenting themselves. Redress for damage thus caused is oftener sought for in equity than at law, yet one case, typical of a large class of suits such as referred to, which came before a court of law, may here be noticed. The complainant sued as for a tort, and after stating the formation of a company for the purpose of smelting and refining the ores of certain mines, and that a certain number of shares therein were to be appropriated and offered to the public at so much per share, alleged that the defendant, intending to defraud, deceive and injure the public, and to cause it to be publicly represented and advertised that the said company was likely to be a safe and profitable undertaking, and also to deceive the public who might become purchasers of the said shares, and to induce them to become such purchasers, falsely, fraudulently and deceitfully caused and procured to be publicly advertised and made known, by prospectus, certain false statements, by means of which the defendant wrongfully and fraudulently induced the plaintiff to become the purchaser and bearer of a large number of shares in the said undertaking, in consequence whereof he incurred loss. To the sufficiency of this complaint objection having been taken, the action was held to be maintainable, as founded upon a false representation, fraudulently made by the defendant to the plaintiff, for the purpose of inducing the plaintiff to act upon it, the plaintiff showing that by so acting upon it he had suffered damage. Under such circumstances, although the parties had been before the particular transaction unknown to each other, an action lies; and it would be strange if a man who has so suffered damage from the wrongful act of another were without remedy.²²²

Fraud is sometimes established at Nisi Prius by putting before the jury an assemblage of facts from which, as reasonable men, the essential ingredient in the right of action may be inferred by them; such assemblage of facts, perhaps, rather raising a presumption than amounting to direct and express proof of *mala fides*. Evidence of this sort has especial force when it brings before the jury the conduct and demeanor of defendant, putting them in such a light as to appear inconsistent with straightforwardness, with rectitude and honesty, or with the real wish to perform a duty. The success of a litigant may be greatly jeopardized by proofs tending to show that in treating as vendor of property with defendants (the purchasers of it), he had "stood by" and allowed them for his own benefit to draw inferences as to the value of the property entirely erroneous, and which, when acted on, proved highly detrimental.²²³

152. From what has been said in the present chapter may be deduced the principal tests for determining whether upon given facts an action of tort be maintainable. Is there proof that a right vested in plaintiff has been infringed by defendant? or that some duty owing by defendant to plaintiff

has been violated or neglected to his damage? Is there proof of anything to justify the act complained of? or to neutralize its apparently tortious character?

Torts not directly affecting the person, reputation, or property of an individual, may nevertheless seriously affect him in some other way; a misrepresentation as to the credit of a stranger may cause ruin to him who relies on it; a malicious act may be equally detrimental to him against whom it is leveled. A breach of duty owing by A. to B., in virtue of some relation subsisting between them, may entail consequences, not too remotely connected with the breach, leading to pecuniary loss and even bankruptcy. Negligence causing death, and so prejudicing relatives who had looked to the deceased person for maintenance and support, negligence causing loss of service to master by reason of bodily hurt done to his servant, may be actionable. The mean and objectionable act of enticing away a man's servant or apprentice may be actionable (Art. 169). For any one of such acts our law is quite willing and able to supply a remedy by awarding, through the intervention of a jury, pecuniary compensation for the damage caused.

I will merely add that the doctrine of ratification may thus be applied in a case of tort. A., professing to act by my authority, does that which, *primâ facie*, is a trespass, and I afterwards assent to and adopt his act. I become a trespasser, as it were, by estoppel, unless I can justify the act. Further, where an act which, if unauthorized, would amount to a trespass has been done in the name and on behalf of another, though without previous authority, the subsequent ratification may enable the party on whose behalf the act was done to take advantage of it, and to treat it as having been done by his direction. Here a rather subtle qualification has to be noticed; the act of ratification must take place at a time and under circumstances when the ratifying party might himself lawfully have done the act which he ratifies.[224]

Further, as regards tort such as treated of and exemplified in the preceding pages, finality has been enforced in part by the statute 21 Jac. I, c. 16, already cited (Art. 105), in part by a strict recognition of the doctrines of merger and estoppel (Art. 106)—by holding that the original cause of action is merged in the judgment of a court of record, and altogether gone—by estopping either party to such judgment or his privies from questioning it in another suit. Judgment recovered as against one of several joint wrong-doers, though unsatisfied, will operate in bar of proceeding against another of them.[225]

CHAPTER VII.

LEGAL PRINCIPLES APPLIED TO TORTS.

"It is a vain thing to imagine a right without a remedy."
LORD HOLT.

153. LORD HOLT's *dictum* has been many times re-echoed, and we have been quite recently told that "where there is a legal right, even against the crown, there must be a legal remedy, and one which can be made effectual."[226] The law will create a remedy fit for the occasion in order that a complainant may not be without redress, should no precedent be found in accordance with which it may be had. In Art. 148, the proposition stated has been strikingly exemplified, and a few additional instances will in this chapter be given to a like effect, showing that our law can apply its old principles to new facts, although, whilst willing and competent to do so, it will not swerve from an observance of established doctrines.

The reader of what follows may amplify the catalogue of cases submitted without limit.

154. A question of much interest amongst farmers and residents in country districts quite recently arose of this kind. An action was brought by the owner of a horse against a person to whom he had sent it to be turned out to pasture, or "agisted," for negligently putting it into a field accessible to a bull, by which it was gored and killed.

The facts were that the defendant, being the owner of marsh land, turned out upon it the plaintiff's horse in company with some heifers, the land being divided from the field where the bull was by a ditch, which the bull could pass, and which he was accustomed to pass in order to visit the heifers. One day the horse was found dead, having evidently been gored by a bull; and the action was brought, not against the owner of the bull, but against the defendant, who agisted the horse, for not taking due care of it, and so allowing it to be gored by the bull. There was no evidence that the bull was used to gore man or beast; on the contrary, witnesses testified that he was really very quiet, but the circumstances attending his attack on plaintiff's horse could not be deposed to. There was evidence showing generally that it was not safe to put bulls and cows in the same field with horses, though some witnesses said that this practice was usual, and that no harm ordinarily came of it. It appeared that bulls are accustomed to stray, so that the defendant ought to have anticipated the probability of the bull coming across the ditch into the same field with the horse, and, indeed, knew that it did so. On this evidence the jury found that there had been a want of due and reasonable care on the part of the defendant in keeping the plaintiff's horse, and awarded substantial damages.

The case standing thus, the action was held to be maintainable upon the ground that the defendant had been negligent in not taking due care of the horse, having put it in a field into which he knew the bull was accustomed to come. "Was that negligence? There was evidence that it was, as a bull is a treacherous animal and of uncertain temper. The law doubtless is that domestic animals, such as bulls and dogs, are not to be regarded by their owners as necessarily dangerous. This rule probably had its origin in times when there were no fences, and cattle were left to wander about on commons and wastes. Therefore, the owner was not liable unless he knew them to be vicious. But it cannot be assumed that these animals are always safe to put other animals with. There is no authority to extend the rule to parties who are bound by contract to take proper care of animals. The defendant in the case put was intrusted with the horse, and bound to take proper care of it, and had failed to do so."

Here, accordingly, the result was adverse to the defendant, albeit another argument was urged on his behalf, *viz.*, that the action should have been brought against the owner of the bull: as to this, however, it was judicially said that if so, the defendant, the agister of the horse, could, under the circumstances mentioned, also sustain an action against the owner of the bull, as the bull wrongfully entered his field. "But then, in such an action against the owner, it would be necessary to show that he knew it to be vicious, so that it would have been more difficult to maintain that action than this; the cause of action for negligence in keeping the horse being quite different from that against the owner of the animal doing the injury."[227]

It will perhaps be thought curious that an ancient head of law, regarding negligence generally, and liability by reason of want of care in the custody of animals domesticated or otherwise in particular, should at this day be appealed to under novel circumstances for determining the rights and liabilities of parties.

---

155. The following case illustrates what has been said in the preceding chapter, and further shows how legal principles may be applied to facts.

The plaintiff deposited with a bank for safe custody a cask containing gold doubloons. It was placed with other deposits in a vault in the bank, and the agent of plaintiff was in the habit of coming to the bank to see that his deposit was secure. The deposit was made solely for the plaintiff's accommodation, and without any advantage thence derivable to the bank. No evidence was given to show how the vault in which the money had been placed was secured: but it appeared that whenever the plaintiff gave orders to the bank, as he often did, for delivering some of the gold doubloons deposited as above mentioned, the cask was opened by the cashier or chief clerk, who delivered the doubloons pursuant to such orders. The cashier and chief clerk, each of whom had previously borne a fair reputation, fraudulently took from the cask doubloons to a large amount, with which they absconded.

Upon these facts the bank was held not responsible to make good the loss, having been guiltless of gross negligence or fraud; "the bank was no more answerable for the act of its officers than it would have been had they stolen the pocket-book of a person who might have laid it upon the counter while he was transacting business at the bank." [225]

The case just cited exemplifies the rule that a

gratuitous bailee is liable only for gross negligence in regard to the thing bailed; and though degrees of care are not well definable, they are, with some approach to certainty, distinguishable, and a jury, under direction of the judge, must try to discriminate as best they may, between degrees of things which run more or less into each other.

156. The plaintiff, suing in a county court, claimed £40 as damages sustained by reason of his cattle being killed through eating the leaves of a yew tree recently felled in defendant's wood adjoining plaintiff's land, and into which the cattle escaped in consequence of defendant's neglect to repair his fence separating the said wood and land. The defendant ought to have maintained the fence in repair. Such being the substance of plaintiff's claim, proofs in support of it were needed to establish these points: 1st, the possession and occupation of the respective lands of plaintiff and defendant; 2dly, the duty of defendant to repair the boundary fence; 3dly, his neglect to do so; 4thly, that the alleged damage accrued to plaintiff, and how it happened.

It appeared in evidence that the defendant had sold to a third person, C., the right to cut down timber in his wood; that C.'s servants cut down a tree there in such a manner that it fell upon and broke the fence separating defendant's land from plaintiff's, and afterwards cut down the yew tree; further, that plaintiff's cattle escaped from his field through the gap in the fence, caused as above mentioned, into defendant's wood, and there ate the leaves of the yew tree which caused their death.

Several interesting questions of law arose upon the above facts. Was the defendant bound, without notice and before the lapse of reasonable time, to repair the fence? Was he liable for damage resulting from the negligence of C.'s servants? Was the damage too remote? The court at Westminster, reversing the decision below, held that the defendant was bound at his peril to maintain at all times, and without notice, a sufficient fence, and that as the damage had not been caused by the act of God (Art. 78) or by *vis major*, he was liable to make it good.

A case founded upon tort more suggestive than this is not perhaps to be found in the reports. Would C., whose servants caused the damage, have been liable to plaintiff? Would C. be liable to recoup defendant in respect of the amount recovered from him at suit of plaintiff?[229]

157. The liability of the owner of a chattel which has to his knowledge some defect in it, to one who, with permission from the owner, uses the chattel and sustains bodily hurt as a consequence of its defective condition, has been sometimes discussed, and its nature and extent have been partially set forth.[230] Such liability, in truth, flows from a breach of duty owing by the owner of the chattel towards him who is to use it, this breach of duty causing damage to the latter. In a case of this kind, difficulty, however, is sometimes felt in determining whether the substantial question involved is one of law or one of fact—of law for the ruling of the judge, of fact for the finding of the jury. Such a difficulty was recently experienced, the facts being as under: The plaintiff, a cab driver, sued the cab proprietor for bodily hurt caused by an unruly horse, which had never been harnessed to a cab, the claim for damages being founded upon breach of duty causing damage. The jury at the first trial of the case found that the horse was not reasonably fit to be driven in a cab, and the plaintiff had a verdict. Whereupon arose a question as to the relation subsisting between plaintiff and defendant; was it that of bailor and bailee, or of master and servant, or was it that of co-adventurers, the liability of the defendant to-

wards plaintiff varying according to the relation between them. After much difference of opinion amongst the judges upon these points, a new trial of the cause was ordered; and at this second trial five questions were submitted to the jury, and amongst them these: Did the plaintiff take the horse and cab wrongfully, or were they intrusted to him by defendant? If so, were they intrusted to him as bailee or as servant? The jury found that they were intrusted to plaintiff as bailee, and the plaintiff again had a verdict, which, after another argument *in banc*, was allowed to stand.[231]

158. A., the owner of certain jewels, puts them in a bag, which is duly sealed and placed by him in the hands of B., a jeweler, for safe custody, B. afterwards breaks the seal, takes the jewels out of the bag, and pledges them to C. for an advance of money. A., being apprised of what has happened, demands the jewels of C., who refuses to give them up, unless upon payment to him of the sum advanced on them.

Upon the facts stated several questions may arise. Is there any, and if so what, civil remedy at suit of A. against C.? To answer this question we must consider: 1st, in what relation B., the jeweler, stood to A.; 2dly, whether or not, or how far, A.

was bound by B.'s act in pawning the jewels? As to the former question, we may conclude that the delivery of the jewels to B. was a bailment of them for the use of the bailor, and that the jeweler was a mere depositary, having no property in the jewels, which could give him a right to sell or dispose of them, but having the custody of them only; 2dly we may conclude that the pledge of the jewels by B. was wrongful, and that the refusal by C. to deliver them up, except on payment of the advance, would vest in A. a right of action against him for their recovery. Consequently A. would have a right to sue C. for the jewels, or their value, quite irrespective of the sum advanced on them; in such a case the jury might assess the value of the jewels conditionally that if they were returned to the plaintiff nominal damages only should be paid.[232] Here, moreover, a presumption *contra spoliatorem* might arise. Should C., having the jewels in his possession, refuse to produce them at the trial, the jury could infer them to be of the finest quality.

A. would have a right of action against B. for the jewels or their value, although in exercising this right difficulty might be encountered by reason of the doctrine of our law already adverted to (Art. 140)—that where a felony has been committed, causing to an individual pecuniary damage, the interest of the public demands that justice should be satisfied before redress by action is sought; and doubtless this rule as to the suspension, rather than the entire merger, of a right of action for a felony practically, in former times, by reason of the law of forfeiture, operated to extinguish the right altogether. Such might not indeed henceforward be its operation, inasmuch as by a recent statute (33 & 34 Vict. c. 23) forfeiture on conviction for felony has been abolished; the property of the convict, though for a time dealt with and administered under the provisions of that act, being, as regards the residue, if any, ultimately restored to him.

Let us observe how the rule specified comes into operation, and what course should be taken when it does so. It may happen that a transaction under investigation at Nisi Prius, and apparently grounded upon tort, is found to involve all the ingredients in an indictable offense. Should such offense be a felony—should the plaintiff, for instance, suing in trespass for assault and battery, or for goods wrongfully taken from him, prove that the defendant had in fact committed in the one case a felonious assault, in the other larceny—the doctrine of our customary law, which has been mentioned, might become operative, and thereupon a question would arise concerning the course to be taken by the judge, the case before him having assumed the aspect indicated. It seems that he could not properly refuse to proceed with the trial, because a Nisi Prius judge is a commissioner appointed by the crown to try such issues as may be brought before him. It rather seems that application should be made on behalf of the defendant to the court out of which the writ issued, at some period antecedent to the trial, to stay proceedings; or that application should be made after verdict to prevent the plaintiff, if successful, from obtaining the fruits of judgment.[233]

Whichever be the right course to be taken under the circumstances supposed, the doctrine alluded to of our common law could not fail to operate adversely to A., in an action for damages brought at his suit against B. Should C., however, be minded to sue B. for the money advanced upon the jewels, C. having had to surrender them to A., their absolute and rightful owner, the doctrine as to merger would not apply; it holds only as between the parties to the principal transaction.

159. A tort of not uncommon occurrence is constituted by the infliction of bodily hurt upon a servant causing damage to his master, by reason of loss of service resulting from the wrongful act and the expense of medical attendance. Such an action

rests upon this basis: that the master has a right to and property in the service of a third person, which right and property have been interfered with by the tortious act of the defendant. Proof of damage is essential to the maintenance of this action. If the hurt were so slight that no loss of service resulted from it, the plaintiff could not recover. The damages are assessed *secundum allegata et probata*. The proofs must follow, and be adapted to the averments made in pleading.

A curious discussion recently arose out of an attempt to extend the operation of the above method of redress. Can a master maintain an action for bodily hurt done to his servant, and causing his immediate death? It may seem strange that for damage and loss of service an action at suit of the master would not in this case lie. When, indeed, the service is simply interrupted by mishap resulting from negligence, the master may recover damages from defendant. But if the service is altogether determined by the same cause, no such action can be sustained. This distinction rests on long continued usage and the general understanding amongst lawyers,[234] recognized in the preamble to Lord Campbell's act (9 & 10 Vict. c. 93).

160. The following case throws light upon the title of the finder of a chattel which has been lost, to retain it for his own use and benefit.

The plaintiff was a traveler for a firm with which the defendant, a shopkeeper, had dealings. The plaintiff called at the defendant's on business, and when leaving the defendant's shop, saw and picked up a parcel lying there on the floor. He showed it to the shopkeeper's assistant, and opening the parcel found that it contained bank notes. The plaintiff then told defendant, who had come into the shop, what he had found, and requested him to keep the notes for delivery to their owner. The defendant accordingly advertised the finding of the notes in the newspapers, stating that they would be restored to their owner on payment of expenses. Three years having elapsed, and no one appearing to claim the notes, plaintiff applied to defendant for them, offering to pay the expense of the advertisements, and to indemnify defendant against any claim which might be made upon him in respect of the notes. Compliance with plaintiff's request having been declined, the question was raised in the county court, had the finder, or had the bailee of the notes the better right to them? The decision was in favor of the plaintiff, for these reasons: The notes had manifestly been lost by some one, and could not, when found, be considered to have been in the defendant's custody, or within the protection of his house; the plaintiff, moreover, by depositing the notes with defendant for a special purpose, did not intend to waive his title to them, and so, although no authority was to be found in our law directly in point, the plaintiff, as against the defendant, was held to have a good title to the notes.[235]

Chattel property may pass into a man's possession without his knowledge, and then, also, a question as to the property, absolute or qualified, in it may arise—as where a man buys a chattel which, unknown to himself and to the vendor, contains valuable property. In a modern case on this subject, a person purchased, at a public auction, a bureau, in a secret drawer of which he afterwards discovered a purse containing money, which he appropriated to his own use. It appeared that, at the time of the sale, no person knew that the bureau contained anything whatever. It was adjudged that, although there was a delivery of the bureau, and a lawful property in it thereby vested in the purchaser, yet that there was no delivery so as to give him a lawful possession of the purse and money as against the vendor, for the vendor had no intention to deliver them, nor the vendee to receive them; both were ignorant of their existence; and when the purchaser discovered that there was a secret drawer containing the purse and money, it was a simple case of finding, and then the law applicable to all cases of finding would apply to this, viz., that the absolute owner of the chattel found is entitled to it as against the finder.[286]

161. A cursory perusal of cases such as collected in the foregoing pages, and a comparison of them with those cited in Chapter V, may convince the reader that legal principles applicable for resolving questions arising out of tort essentially differ from rules of law which become familiar to us in connection with contract. Tort is more akin to crime than to contract, and is so regarded in our legal literature.

CHAPTER VIII.

A CRIME—WHAT IT IS.

Criminal law "merits, for reasons too obvious to be enlarged on, the attention of every man living. For no rank, no elevation in life, and no conduct, how circumspect soever, ought to tempt a reasonable man to conclude that these inquiries do not, nor possibly can, concern him. A moment's cool reflection on the utter instability of human affairs, and the numberless unforeseen effects which a day may bring forth, will be sufficient to guard any man, conscious of his own infirmities, against a delusion of this kind."—SIR M. FOSTER.

"Les lois ne se chargent de punir que les actions extérieures."
MONTESQUIEU.

162. EACH member of society should know the duties owing by him to the public and to individuals, and should be able to recognize his responsibilities. This is especially true as regards the law of crimes. If civil procedure and matters regulated by it are worthy of attention, so, *a fortiori*, should be studied and understood the principles of crown law, which controls and governs the members of each class of society, and knows no distinction between ranks.

Assuming, then, that each of us should be able to appreciate the doctrines of that coercive law under which he lives, I propose to inquire concerning them, first smoothing away preliminary difficulties, and then briefly noticing *seriatim* the principal ingredients in crime.

163. To the question, what is a "criminal act?" the answer most generally applicable seems to be—a criminal act is one which in some way or other subjects the actor to punishment. If the doer of a specified act is visited with a penalty in the shape of a pecuniary fine, and in default of payment thereof, with imprisonment, we shall be justified in saying that the act specified is criminal; and why so? Because imprisonment is in contemplation of law a most severe punishment, for the law esteems highly the liberty of the subject, and so, from the nature of the punishment, we may infer the character and quality of the act to which it is annexed.[237]

The answer to the question put—what sort of act is criminal?—cannot assuredly be regulated by reference to queries such as these. Is it summarily punishable? Is it a misdemeanor? Is it a felony? As regards the first of these queries, although very many cases are summarily disposed of by a single magistrate, or at petty sessions, with a view to economizing time and money, yet they are dealt with in accordance with the principles of law observed at quarter sessions and the assizes; and an act may in its nature be criminal though not indictable. Then as regards the second and third of the queries suggested, the distinction between felonies and misdemeanors is very arbitrary, and can afford no clue for determining whether an act charged to be an indictable offense is *per se* criminal.

164. In order to determine with certainty, irrespective of the general test above indicated, the nature of a crime, we must search for the ingredients in it, and we shall find that a crime is constituted by an overt act done with a guilty intent, or includes a guilty mind, knowledge, or possession, affecting or prejudicing the public. These ingredients in crime will be commented on in due order.

165. The nature of an overt act, criminal and punishable, will be exemplified in almost every page of this chapter; the persuading an apprentice to embezzle his master's goods would be an act cognizable by the law,[238] and any such act must generally be proved in the Crown Court, as at Nisi Prius.

Be it observed, however, *in limine*, that although a fact must be established by the same proofs in criminal as in civil procedure, the legal inference deducible from a fact proved at Nisi Prius may be quite different from the inference deducible from the same fact evidenced in a criminal prosecution.

Thus the fact that A. was agent for B. must be

proved by like evidence at a criminal as at a civil trial, but it will not follow that B. will incur criminal responsibility for the act of A. because he might be civilly answerable for it. The mode of proof is one thing, the effect of the evidence is another.

If a man employs an agent for a perfectly legal purpose, and his agent does an illegal act, that act does not affect the principal, unless it is shown that the principal directed the agent so to act, or really meant he should so act, or afterwards ratified the illegal act, or unless it be shown that the principal appointed one to be his general agent to do both legal and illegal acts.[239] If, however, a person, though resident abroad, do, through the medium of an agent, an act in this country here punishable, the principal so offending might be made answerable to our laws should he come afterwards within their reach.

A master, as we have seen, is civilly answerable for the negligent act of his servant causing bodily hurt to complainant, if the servant, when guilty of the breach of duty imputed, was acting in the service of the master, and in the course of his regular and accustomed duty (Art. 75). In such a case, if the death of the injured person ensued, the servant might be indictable for manslaughter, but the master could not be made criminally answerable, because there would be no felonious or criminal intent proved as against him; unless, indeed, the master ordered his servant to do the particular act, or to do something which naturally caused the death, or unless the master could be brought within the definition of an "accessory before the fact"— *i. e.*, one who, being absent at the time of the particular felony committed, did procure, counsel, command, or abet another to commit it.

If the driver of a coach maliciously upsets it, and so causes hurt to a passenger, the coach proprietor being at the time absent, this latter party may nevertheless be civilly liable for the damage caused, and though the servant might expose himself to an indictment, the master would not be criminally responsible. Here an express statutory provision (24 & 25 Vict. c. 100, s. 35) might apply, so as to render that person criminally amenable, and that person only, whose act had done the harm. This section enacts that "whosoever having the charge of any carriage" shall, "by wanton or furious driving" . . . "or other willful misconduct, or by willful neglect, do or cause to be done any bodily harm" to another shall be guilty of a misdemeanor.

Consistently with what has been just said, penal consequences are not in general incurred for non-observance of statutory requirements where there has been no personal neglect or default by the party charged; *ex. gr.*, the owner of a colliery is required to observe certain precautions and regulations in regard to the use by the miners of safety lamps; should he appoint a competent person to examine and deliver these lamps to the miners, the owner will not be liable to a penalty in respect of the act or default of the person so employed by him, though it be in contravention of the statute law.[240]

166. Generally speaking, then, a fact may be proven in the Crown Court in like manner as it is provable at Nisi Prius; as regards, however, the sufficiency and stringency of the proofs adduced in crown procedure, they must be brought very closely home to—and tell very conclusively against—the accused in order that a conviction may be had.

Let us suppose that in an action against a carrier for the loss of plaintiff's goods, an issue is raised whether the loss arose from the felonious act of the carrier's servants, an issue which, if found for the plaintiff, would entitle him to a verdict.[241] It would suffice for the plaintiff to show facts rendering it more probable that the felony was committed by some one or other of the carrier's servants than by a person not in his employ. Far more stringent proof than this would, however, be needed, if a charge of larceny were preferred against a particular servant or particular servants of the defendant;[212] for the weight of evidence, and of proofs legally admissible adduced against a person accused of crime ought to be such that, to justify conviction, twelve men of average intelligence should believe him to be guilty.

167. In arguing by analogy from the mode of proof in civil procedure, a practitioner in the Crown Court must be somewhat wary; though such a course of reasoning may often be relied on.

Where the question is as to the effect of a written instrument, the instrument itself is primary evidence of its contents, and until it is produced, or its non-production is excused, no secondary evidence of them can be received (Art. 85); this rule holding in criminal and in civil suits. Recently, this principle was relied on as excluding a presumption of guilty knowledge, drawn from the fact that defendant had attempted to commit a fraud similar to that for which he was indicted, by passing as genuine a ring set with false diamonds, the ring not being produced in court. The judges, however, in repudiating this objection, argued by analogy from civil procedure. There is no case, they said, deciding that when the issue is as to the state of a chattel, the soundness of a horse, or the equality of the bulk of goods to the sample, the chattel produced in court constitutes primary evidence, so that no other evidence can be given till the chattel has been inspected by the jury; *ergo*, it would not be incumbent on counsel for the prosecution, under the circumstances put, to produce the ring, witnesses being called to speak to the attempted fraud.[213]

168. The ingredient, then, in crime first to be specified is an overt act—the act being criminal and punishable at common law, or made so expressly or impliedly by statute. In affixing to such an act its precise technical quality, character and designation, difficulty may occur; and in saying whether, upon facts deposed to, this or that offense has been committed. The Legislature, moreover, has sometimes deemed it necessary to declare an indictable act which might or might not have been within the reach and cognizance of our customary law; in so doing it more or less minutely and circumstantially defines the offense constituted, leaving other states of facts not precisely falling within the letter of its enactment to be dealt with by the common law. Under such circumstances, where the statute applies, the indictment is framed upon the statute, and should the proofs fail to bring the case within it, a conviction may still possibly be had at common law.

A statute may directly prohibit or may prohibit indirectly by affixing a penalty to the doing of a particular thing. And in construing a penal statute this fundamental rule must be kept in mind; such an act is to be construed strictly.[244]

169. In Arts. 17, 164, certain characteristics of a crime have been noticed: (1) it concerns or affects the public; and (2) it is prejudicial, or threatens to be so, to the community.

(1) The enticing away of plaintiff's servant might constitute a grievous wrong, and so be actionable; it was, however, long since held (*temp.* Queen Anne) not to be indictable, the wrong done being in its nature private, rather than one affecting the community. Every violation of the law, it was argued, is *in malum exemplum*, but not therefore necessarily indictable.[245]

That an act criminal and punishable concerns the public will be amply exemplified ere this chapter is concluded.

(2) The quality of an act may have to be determined by marking its effect on the community at large. An indictment is a brief narrative of an offense which the public good requires should be punished; and the question—Is such or such an act indictable? may necessitate an inquiry of this kind: What is the tendency of the act as regards the public—is it of evil example? and so forth (Arts. 11 *et seq.*). Considerations of convenience, expediency,

and public policy may thus weigh with our judges in deciding whether a transaction brought before them in purely criminal procedure does really afford ground for an indictment. The uttering of a forged testimonial to character by one knowing it to be forged is a misdemeanor at common law, the intent of defendant found by the jury being to deceive and so to obtain a situation of emolument, and the forging of such a document would likewise be an offense at common law;[246] which may have been violated so that punishment will ensue, although the misdemeanant was not actuated in what he did by any wrongful or improper motive.[247]

A magistrate accordingly called on to convict summarily, or to commit for trial an accused person, may need closely to regard the quality of the act charged against him.

170. An act deemed criminal by our law is almost always found, when analyzed, to have been done with a guilty mind (*mens rea*) or intention, or to have been accompanied with a guilty knowledge or possession.

171. In general, that which our law designates as criminal, and deems punishable, is an act done with a criminal intent. The act and the intention must concur to constitute a crime, nor amongst offenses indictable at common law does any very

material exception offer itself to this rule. Our law, indeed, holds that where owing to immaturity of years, or the sanitary condition of the person implicated, there can be no intention, there can be no crime; no act coming within the reach of our criminal law can be done. And our courts will, if possible, construe statutory words, without doing violence to them, in accordance with the rule which has been mentioned. The *mens rea*, it has been judicially observed, "is an essential ingredient in an offense. It is true it may be dispensed with by statute, but the terms which should induce us (the judges) to infer that it is dispensed with must be very strong."[248] To punish one who acted with an innocent intention, or under an innocent belief as to the quality of his act, might appear under any circumstances hard, did we not remember that an act in itself indifferent is sometimes, for the protection of the revenue, for the security of traders or otherwise, forbidden and made punishable, and that every man is bound to know the law.

Simple instances, showing how essential the intent may be as a constituent element in a statutory crime are such as these:

By statute (24 & 25 Vict. c. 100, s. 31), whosoever shall set, or cause to be set, any engine calculated to destroy human life, or inflict grievous bodily harm with the intent that the same "may destroy or inflict grievous bodily harm upon a trespasser or other person coming in contact therewith," shall be guilty of a misdemeanor. To support an indictment upon this statutory provision, the intent of the alleged transgressor must be proved; it will have to be inferred from circumstances such as the position of the gun or other instrument, the declarations of defendant, and so forth.

One particular kind of cheating, by the use of fraudulent wrappers, is now provided for by statute (25 & 26 Vict. c. 88); pursuant to sect. 3 of which any person who, with intent to defraud, shall apply a forged or counterfeit trade-mark to any label with which a chattel is to be sold or exposed for sale, is made guilty of a misdemeanor; and other provisions have been inserted in this statute with a view to repressing the practice, which had become prevalent, of imposing on the public and damaging individuals by frauds analogous to that mentioned. Proof of the intent to defraud would be material to support an indictment under any one of such statutory clauses.

172. If it be asked how, at a trial in the Crown Court, the intent of the party charged is to be discovered? I reply: By the facts themselves; by the precedent, concomitant, and subsequent circum-

stances, by the manner of doing the principal act, and the like. For instance, if the indictment were for wounding with intent to murder, framed upon the stat. 24 & 25 Vict. c. 100 (s. 18), the kind of weapon used would be material, the force and violence with which it was used, the lying in wait, and so forth. If the means employed were appropriate for accomplishing the result charged, the jury will have to say whether that result was within the intention and design of the accused.

If, moreover, from the overt acts constituting and circumstances attending the alleged crime, the requisite intention cannot with sufficient certainty be deduced or implied, other acts of the prisoner similar to that under investigation may, in some cases, have to be submitted to the jury, as showing more conclusively the intent. Thus, on an indictment for arson, it being doubtful whether the burning was by accident or by design, proof has been admitted that at some other time the prisoner intentionally attempted to set fire to the same building as that specified in the indictment.[249]

173. The difficulty of proving the intent with which an act was done being great and peculiar, a presumption is *ex necessitate* held permissible of this kind—a man must be taken to be answerable for that which he knows to be the ordinary conse-

quence of what he does or expressly permits.[259] Where a man is charged with doing a wrongful act, of which the probable consequence may be highly injurious, without legal justification, the intention is an inference of law from the doing of the act. And although the accused person may have had a different object in view, he must be taken to have intended that which is the natural consequence of the act.

If a man does an act which is illegal, the act is not rendered legal merely by the fact that it was done with a legal object. Unless the object were such as rendered the particular act lawful, there is no legal excuse disclosed for doing the act. Let us suppose such a case as this: The law says that matter of a certain kind or tendency shall not be published—matter such as prohibited is, however, published, though with an ulterior intention of benefiting the public. Circumstances, nevertheless, show that the person doing this act must have known that it would produce the consequences contemplated by the Legislature as likely to flow from it, and meant to be repressed. Is the actor justified in doing that which clearly would be wrong, legally as well as morally, because he thinks that some counterbalancing or greater good may be accomplished by the doing of it? The answer to this question is, "You shall not do evil that good may come."[251]

174. Although a criminal intent must usually accompany an act, in order that the full legal conception of crime may be satisfied, this rule is subject to qualification, for a bare act is sometimes made indictable by statute; and where an act of violence, involving a breach of the peace, is committed, the inquiry as to intent may be superfluous.

In the forgery act (24 & 25 Vict. c. 98) is contained this provision (s. 17): whosoever, without lawful authority or excuse (the proof whereof shall lie on the party accused), shall engrave upon any plate any word, the impression taken from which "shall resemble, or apparently be intended to resemble," any part of a note of the Bank of England, shall be guilty of felony. To convict under this section, it would suffice to prove the doing of the particular act specified, which proof would be answered by showing lawful authority or excuse for doing it.

To some crimes of violence reference will presently be made.

175. Proof of a guilty knowledge may be needed to justify conviction for crime; and when such proof is added to and combined with proof of possession, not satisfactorily explained, it may go far

towards insuring a verdict against the accused person.

The policy of our Legislature has wisely been to make guilty knowledge or guilty possession an essential element in each of certain acts which have to be repressed, prevented, or punished. Here can only be given a few instances in aid of what has been said—a perusal of recent statutes concerning criminal law would supply very many more.

It has been held that a person cannot be convicted under s. 8 of 6 & 7 Will. IV, c. 37, for using prohibited ingredients in the making of bread for sale, unless there be knowledge either in himself, or in the person employed by him, of the presence of the ingredients; a guilty knowledge, coupled with possession, constituting the offense thus made punishable.[252]

Guilty knowledge is also an essential ingredient in the offense of keeping a diseased animal in one's possession, without giving notice to the police, as required by statute 32 & 33 Vict. c. 70, s. 75, and by an order issued by the privy council pursuant thereto.[253]

Again, a summary conviction may be had against any man having in his possession, or on his premises, with his knowledge, an engine for taking deer, unless he can show that he had a lawful occasion for the same, and did not keep it for an unlawful purpose. Here the possession *scienter* is made punishable; and it will be for the justice to determine whether the defendant had lawful occasion for the engine, and whether he kept it or not for an unlawful purpose.

176. In general where the possession of a thing is made indictable and punishable, the guilty knowledge or *scienter* is expressly or constructively made an ingredient in the offense charged against the prisoner, and proofs of guilty or criminal possession must be adduced on the part of the prosecution, in order that a conviction may be had.

Thus, by sect. 14 of the forgery act (24 & 25 Vict. c. 98), whosoever, without lawful authority or excuse, the proof whereof shall lie on the party accused, shall knowingly have in his custody or possession paper water-marked in a certain manner shall be guilty of felony. Here the *scienter* is expressly made an ingredient in the crime. Proof of the *scienter* is sometimes held to be necessary by construction—by a perusal of other parts of the act containing the provision on which the indictment has been framed, and by gathering therefrom the intention of the Legislature.

It is enacted, by sect. 24 of the act last cited, that whosoever without lawful authority or excuse, the proof whereof shall lie on the party accused, shall have in his custody or possession any press for coinage, knowing such press to be a press for coinage, shall be guilty of felony. To support an indictment framed upon this section, it would only be necessary to show that the thing specified was in the custody or possession, according to the statutory significance of those words (see sect. 1), of the accused person—also the guilty knowledge. It would be for the prisoner to show that he had lawful authority or excuse for the possession of the thing specified, which possession is *primâ facie* made illegal.

177. Sometimes, by reason of the difficulty of proving a particular ingredient in a crime, our Legislature has, so to speak, relieved the jury from the perplexity in which they might find themselves at a trial for that offense, by empowering them to convict without proof being adduced of the presence in the criminal act charged of such ingredient. And of late years, since our penal code has become milder, this course seems to have been more freely adopted than of old.

Thus by sect. 5 of the stat. 24 & 25 Vict. c. 99, which concerns offenses relating to the coinage, it is enacted that whosoever shall unlawfully have in his custody or possession any gold or silver bullion which shall have been produced or obtained by impairing any of the queen's current gold or silver coin, knowing the same to have been so produced or obtained, shall be guilty of felony. Before this enactment became operative, it frequently happened that filings, chippings, and gold dust were found under circumstances which left no doubt that they had been produced by impairing coin—evidence being, nevertheless, wanting to prove that any particular coin had been impaired. The difficulty which had thus sometimes been experienced in adducing apt and sufficient evidence, under circumstances such as indicated, was by this statutory provision removed.

There can be no doubt that legislative intervention such as referred to, which facilitates the performance of their functions by a jury, without unfairly embarrassing the accused, is beneficial, and prevents lamentable failures of justice such as formerly occurred.

178. Where the guilty knowledge of an accused person is an essential ingredient in the offense with which he stands charged, it may sometimes be necessary to examine as to collateral facts, with a view to establishing such knowledge. Thus in the course of a prosecution for passing counterfeit money, the fact that the accused, when apprehended, had other

counterfeit money about him, is admissible in evidence to show a guilty knowledge—to show that the accused knew that the money which he is charged with uttering was counterfeit.

That such a mode of proof is, under the circumstances, properly admitted—that the inference deducible from the fact deposed to may be safely drawn —seems to have been recognized by the Legislature; for by s. 10 of the act which concerns offenses relating to the coinage (24 & 25 Vict. c. 99) it is enacted that whosoever shall utter false or counterfeit coin, having at the time any other such coin in his "custody or possession" shall be guilty of a misdemeanor, and be much more severely punishable than one who is convicted merely of the uttering of counterfeit coin. By this enactment, accordingly, a criminal course of conduct is to be inferred from the possession of spurious or counterfeit money. And hence questions having reference to such possession would be relevant, and might properly be put by counsel to the witnesses for the crown upon the trial of an indictment for uttering base coin.

179. When the fact that the accused person did the act charged against him is proved—as that he passed a forged document or base coin, or attempted to obtain goods by false pretenses—proof of the

guilty knowledge may be by showing that shortly before the principal transaction the accused was pursuing a course of similar acts, raising a presumption that the act charged was not done under a mistake, but that the quality of it was known to the accused.

So, the possession of property, shown to have been stolen from the prosecutor, shortly after the theft was committed, is held to afford strong and reasonable ground of presumption that the person in whose possession the stolen property is found was the real thief, unless he can account for the fact of its being in his possession in some way consistently with his innocence. Possession of the fruits of crime, under circumstances such as supposed, is *primâ facie* evidence of guilty possession, and, if unexplained, is usually regarded by a jury as conclusive; the question, what amounts to recent possession varying according as the stolen article is or is not calculated to pass readily from hand to hand, or otherwise.

180. Criminal acts may be viewed in like order as tortious acts have been noticed, and, this mode of treatment being adopted, a comparison of the former with the latter is readily to be made. The main ingredient in a crime may be violence directed against the person or property; it may be consti-

tuted by breach of duty, negligence, malice or fraud. In the following articles each such species of acts, criminal and punishable, will be exemplified by reference to crimes of common occurrence.

181. An act done forcibly and illegally to a man's person or property, such and so done as to threaten the peace or prejudice the welfare of the community, may be indictable.

182. Murder, we know, is homicide done feloniously, willfully, and of malice aforethought; and manslaughter is homicide done feloniously, without malice: either of these acts being very hurtful to the community. These definitions being regarded, we shall find that an indictment for murder contains within it, substantially a charge of manslaughter, aggravated by an averment of malice, and therefore it is that a conviction for the minor of these two offenses may be had upon an indictment which charges and sets forth the major of them.

The *onus* lies necessarily on the prosecution of proving the case against the person accused of murder, and in doing so, it will be incumbent on counsel for the crown to make out the case as fully as possible against him, so as to relieve the jury from doubt respecting his guilt, and further, to support their verdict when given, and the sentence of the court upon it. Should, indeed, the facts proved on a trial for murder, show that the death was caused by the accused, the presumption of law is against him; he will be presumed to have acted maliciously, and he will have to exculpate himself as best he may from the charge thus *primâ facie* established. It will be for the prisoner to reduce the homicide in degree, and this he may do through his counsel, either by analyzing and reasoning on the case for the prosecution, or by adducing new facts in explanation or in partial disproof of it.

Where homicide occurs in the absence of any third person who can directly testify to it, it nevertheless often happens that facts are adducible in some way implicating the prisoner. He was last seen with the deceased; he had before the occurrence expressed enmity towards him; he was seen coming from the place where the transaction had occurred; the state of his dress or person was such as to provoke suspicion; thus circumstantial evidence may satisfy a jury that homicide has been done, and done by the accused, and it will then be for him to exonerate himself from the suspicion attaching to him. The presumption of law just noticed applies; homicide brought home to a person is murder, unless shown to have been justifiable or excusable, or reduced in quality and degree.

It may and often does happen that the accused person, when first charged with an offense such as spoken of, makes a statement which admits the homicide but goes to show that it was excusable; he will, *a fortiori*, have to encounter the presumption which has been referred to. He will have to convince the jury that the statement put forward is credible and trustworthy, and that appearances against him are fallacious, and explicable in a manner consistent with his innocence. Experience has shown how difficult it is for one conscious of his guilt, and suddenly charged with it, at once, on the spur of the moment, to concoct a story which shall be truthlike, not overstrained or artificial, and shall be free from discrepancies which might be fatal to the defense afterwards set up.

On a trial for murder, the proofs adduced may be such as to necessitate either a conviction for that crime or an acquittal; should, however, the facts deposed to justify a verdict of guilty of manslaughter, the proper mode of dealing with them will be explained to the jury by the judge.

183. With a view to realizing the mode of proof that an indictable offense involving force has been committed, let us suppose that the prisoner stands charged with robbery—a crime somewhat peculiar and technical in its nature. Let us very

shortly define this offense, note the averments in the indictment charging it, the proofs for the prosecution and the grounds of defense which might be relied on.

Robbery, it has been judicially said,[254] is the stealing or taking from the person of another, or in the presence of another, of property, with such a degree of force or fear as to induce the owner unwillingly to part with it; and whether fear arises from real or expected violence to the person, or from a sense of injury to the character, matters not in legal contemplation; for to most men the idea of losing their good fame and reputation is as terrifying as the dread of personal injury. "The principal ingredient in robbery is a man's being forced to part with his property."

Such being the definition of the offense of robbery, the averments in the indictment charging it are: that the accused in and upon one A. feloniously did make an assault, and him, the said A., in bodily fear and danger of his life feloniously did put, and the moneys of the said A. (to such an amount) from his person and against his will feloniously did steal. The putting in fear is a special ingredient in the crime of robbery, as to which Sir Michael Foster observes,[255] that for the prosecution it must be shown either that the prosecutor was actually in fear from the defendant's actions at the time alleged, or else circumstances must be shown from which may be presumed such a degree of apprehension of danger as would induce the prosecutor to part with his property; though if the circumstances proved be such as are calculated to create that degree of fear, the court will not further pursue the inquiry to ascertain whether the fear actually existed. If a man be suddenly knocked down and stripped of his property while senseless, he cannot in strictness be said to be put in fear, yet this would undoubtedly be a robbery.

In support of a prosecution for robbery the proofs, we may suppose, would be in part direct, consisting, *inter alia*, of the evidence of the prosecutor, in part circumstantial: the prisoner was seen near the place spoken of shortly before the act was done; he was found in possession of the fruits of crime; he made, when questioned or apprehended, statements, as to such possession or otherwise, proved to have been false.

If, on such a trial as supposed, the case for the crown being closed, there appear but a mere *scintilla* of evidence against the accused, which, in the opinion of the judge, would not justify or sustain a verdict of "guilty," the jury will be directed to acquit. If, on the close of the whole case, facts have become apparent as well in favor of as against the prisoner, it will be for the jury, after the judge has summed up and commented upon the evidence, to balance the conflicting probabilities, and, should there be a reasonable doubt as to his innocence, give to the accused the benefit of such doubt.

On a trial for robbery the jury may, perhaps, on balancing the evidence *pro* and *con.* come to the conclusion that no actual robbery was committed, but that there was an assault with intent to rob; if so, they may return as their verdict "guilty" of such an assault, and the prisoner will thereupon be punishable as if he had been convicted upon an indictment charging it.[256] A provision of this kind is meant to prevent a serious delay, if not a failure, in the administering of justice, and can in no respect prejudice the prisoner, for, by the statutory terms used in the section referred to, no person tried for robbery shall, if acquitted, be afterwards liable to be prosecuted for an assault with intent to commit the same robbery.

184. Let us now take a case of burglary, and treat it briefly in the manner just adopted, defining the offense, noticing the form of the indictment which charges it, and then considering the proofs adducible in support of, and in answer to, the charge.

Lord Coke[257] defines a burglar to be he who by night breaketh and entereth into a mansion house, or, we may say, "dwelling-house," with intent to commit a felony.

In defining the word "dwelling-house," we are aided by the Legislature (24 & 25 Vict. c. 96, s. 53), it being enacted that "no building, although within the same curtilage with any dwelling-house, and occupied therewith, shall be deemed to be part of such dwelling-house" for any of the purposes of the act, unless there be "a communication between such building and dwelling-house either immediate or by means of a covered and inclosed passage leading from the one to the other." So in regard to "night time" occurring in Lord Coke's definition, the practitioner is again assisted by the Legislature, which, for the purposes of the act just cited, enacts (s. 1), that the night shall be deemed to commence at nine o'clock in the evening, and to terminate at six o'clock in the succeeding day.

Let us next notice the form of the indictment for burglary, prefacing that the charges contained in it may be of breaking and entering with intent to commit a felony, or may, in addition to this, allege that an actual felony was committed; whether the felony be such at common law or by statute matters not, neither does it signify what felony it be, though in practice the felony contemplated or committed is almost always larceny. The indictment then charges that the accused, "the dwelling-house of A., situate at [such a place], feloniously and burglariously did break and enter, with intent the goods and chattels of one B., in the said dwelling-house then being, feloniously and burglariously to steal, take and carry away, and then in the said dwelling-house [such and such things] of the goods and chattels of the said B., of the value of [£5], in the said dwelling-house then being found, feloniously and burglariously did steal, take and carry away," &c.

In this indictment the word "burglariously" must appear: it is a technical word, known to our customary law, for which no other expression may be substituted.

To the words "break and enter" an extended significance has been given by the Legislature; for in virtue of the 51st section of the larceny act (24 & 25 Vict. c. 96), the entry may be before the breaking as well as after it. "Whosoever shall enter the dwelling-house of another with intent to commit any felony therein, or being in such dwelling-house shall commit any felony therein, and shall, in either case, break out of the said dwelling-house in the night, shall be deemed guilty of burglary." We thus perceive that the common law definition of burglary given by Lord Coke must now be considered amplified and altered; a class of offenders not less dangerous than burglars, as defined by him, having been brought within reach of the punishment ensuing on a conviction for this crime; the breaking out of the dwelling-house must, however, to satisfy the statutory words, be in the night time.

What, in the next place, is a "breaking" and an "entering"—words contained in the indictment for burglary? To satisfy the word "break," there must in general be, not a mere legal trespass, as by passing over an invisible boundary, but a substantive and forcible irruption. If a person leaves his house door or his window open, and a man enters thereby, this is no burglary, because the word "break" in the indictment is not satisfied—the householder has but his own folly and negligence to blame. Yet to a case such as specified, a clause in the larceny act[258] might be applicable, under which any person found by night in a dwelling-house with intent to commit a felony therein, is guilty of a misdemeanor, and may be punished even with penal servitude.

In support of an indictment for burglary very slight proof of a breaking may suffice—the lifting up of the latch of a door or the sash of a window will do so.[239] And competent authorities affirm that an entry into a house effected down a chimney is sufficient, for the mode of access is as much closed as the nature of things will permit.

' As to the entry, little difficulty can be felt—the stepping over the threshold of a house, or the putting the hand in at a window to extract goods, may constitute a burglarious entry.

Lastly, on a trial for burglary, doubt cannot in general be felt by a jury as to the intent. If an actual felony, no matter what, was committed in the house, an intent to commit that, or some other specified felony, may be presumed, the ordinary incentive to burglary being the larcenous taking of goods and chattels.

It may, however, chance that although the entire charge contained in the indictment has not been made out, some substantive portion of it, separable as it were from the rest, has been established. What, then, is the course to be pursued? The charge exhibited in the indictment for burglary is, in truth, composite; and if, on the trial of an indictment for this felony, charging the commission of theft, the proofs for the crown have failed to show that the breaking and entry were in the night time, but have sufficed to show that there was a breaking and entry, and that goods, say to the value of £5, were stolen, a conviction for house-breaking might ensue. If the proofs failed to show the breaking and entering, a conviction for stealing in a dwelling-house to the amount of £5 might be had. If the fact of a breaking and that of an entry were established, but no actual larceny were shown to have been committed, a conviction might be had for breaking and entering the dwelling-house with intent to commit a felony therein. The discretionary power thus given to a jury may be beneficially exercised to prevent justice from being for a time defeated, and to save delay and expense in administering it.

185. The offense of simple larceny consists in the taking and carrying away of the chattel property of another with a felonious intent to convert it to the taker's own use, or to deprive the owner permanently of it. The indictment for this offense charges that the prisoner such and such of the goods and chattels of the prosecutor "feloniously did steal, take and carry away," and the proofs for the crown on a trial for simple larceny must establish: (1) a taking; (2) a felonious intent; (3) a carrying away, technically termed an "asportation."

(1) To constitute larceny at common law there must be a taking—a manual assumption of the chattel in question—against the will of its owner; there must be an act of trespass, so that, if a person ac-

cused of stealing were guilty of no trespass in taking the goods, he could not be guilty of felony in carrying them away; and again, to support a charge of larceny the prosecutor must have had such a possession of the thing taken as would have enabled him to maintain an action of trespass against one who took it without a felonious intent.

By our common law, then, a chattel alleged to have been stolen must have been obtained against the will of its owner. Where a chattel had been bailed to another, or where it had passed to him under and in pursuance of a contract, wherever indeed the property alleged to have been stolen came into the hands of the accused rightfully in the first instance, and without any *animus furandi*, a subsequent wrongful appropriation of the chattel could not, at common law, have constituted larceny. If A. lends B. a horse, or sends goods by a carrier, and the bailee in either case makes off with them, this is at common law no larceny. But if, in the latter case, the bale of goods be opened and a portion of them be thence wrongfully abstracted, or if the conveyance of the goods be fully accomplished, and they are afterwards tortiously converted, the case is different, inasmuch as the bailment was determined by the tortious act, or by performance of the trust, so that a constructive possession became thus revested in the bailor.

The law in regard to larceny by a bailee has been amended by various sections of the larceny act (24 & 25 Vict. c. 96), from amongst which reference may especially be made to sect. 3, enacting that whosoever "being a bailee of any chattel, money, or valuable security, shall fraudulently take or convert the same to his own use, or the use of any person other than the owner thereof, though he shall not break bulk or otherwise determine the bailment, shall be guilty of larceny." This section, accordingly, gets rid of the technical difficulties in the way of convicting a bailee of larceny at common law resulting from the theory that larceny involves a trespass, a taking; and that where goods had passed to the bailee with the bailor's consent, there was no evidence of a taking. Even at common law, however, fraud practiced by the accused person might so operate as to nullify the apparent consent of the owner to parting with the property in his goods. For instance, if the prosecutor had been tricked out of the possession of a thing, and had no intention of parting with the property in it, if the transaction which would naturally have terminated in a transfer of such property were incomplete, the accused going away with the chattel and appropriating it to his own use, might be convicted of larceny.[260]

(2) To constitute larceny at common law, a felonious intent must accompany the taking, "felonious" being a technical word applicable in early times to offenses which, with few exceptions, were capitally punishable, and a conviction for which entailed forfeiture (Art. 158). At the present day, our criminal law having been consolidated and amended, misdemeanors, some of them more serious and more severely visited than many felonies, have been defined or created by the Legislature.

A felony being deemed a very heinous crime, the presumption of law was under certain circumstances strongly in favor of one accused of it. Our law, indeed, always presumes that a person charged with having done a criminal act is innocent until the contrary be proved; and sometimes it does not allow of evidence to counteract this presumption. A married woman stealing in the presence of her husband is presumed to do so under his coercion, though facts of rare occurrence might be received to prove her guilt. It is a presumption of law that an infant within the age of seven years cannot conceive a felonious intent, and no evidence of precocity would avail by way of answer to this presumption. If, however, an infant between the age of seven and that of fifteen years commits felony, the presumption of law, although in his favor, may be rebutted by evidence of malice or of a mischievous discretion.

Regard being had to this component ingredient—a felonious intent—in the crime of larceny, an indictment charging it, could not be founded on a mere careless taking away of another's goods, for to constitute larceny, there must be an intent to "steal,"—a technical word indicative of the offense, and indispensable in the indictment—which involves a knowledge that the property taken does not belong to the taker; and if all the facts concerning the title to a chattel are known to the accused, so that it becomes a pure question of law whether the property in it is his or not, still he may show that he honestly thought it his through a misapprehension of law. And hence into the definition of larceny is sometimes introduced this condition—that the taking must not be justified by any color of title, nor be made in the assertion of a right. For although ignorance of our criminal code could not be set up successfully in answer to a charge of larceny, ignorance of the law of property might be relied upon to give an innocent color and complexion to a taking which, if unexplained, might seem to be larcenous and felonious.

It will, therefore, be the duty of counsel for the prisoner on a trial for larceny—the fact of the taking being proved—to contend, should there be a particle of evidence in support of such contention, that the taking was not felonious, that it occurred through mistake or carelessness, or in assertion of a right, or with intent to restore the thing taken, after it had served some casual purpose, to its lawful owner.

Counsel for the defense may also perhaps successfully contend, where the thing alleged to have been stolen was originally bailed to the prisoner, that there was no taking of it, and nothing done to satisfy the statutory provision already cited as sometimes applicable in such a case. Recently a person was indicted for larceny as bailee of a coat. The evidence showed that the prosecutor had lent the coat to the prisoner to wear for a day, and some few days afterwards the prisoner was found wearing the coat on board a vessel bound for Australia. It was held that no proof appeared of a conversion sufficient to satisfy the statute, for "the determination of the bailment must be something analogous to larceny, and some act must be done inconsistent with the purposes of the bailment."[261]

(3) Further, to constitute the crime of larceny, the thing in question must have been carried away,

or, in technical language, there must have been an asportation of it by the prisoner. About this, however, there can in general be little difficulty, for a bare removal of the chattel from the place in which he found it, though the thief does not quite make off with it, is a sufficient asportation to satisfy the law word "*asportavit*" formerly used in the indictment for larceny. If a man be leading another's horse out of a field, and be apprehended in the fact, or if a guest stealing goods out of an inn has removed them from his chamber down stairs, either proof would suffice to sustain the allegation of *asportavit*.

Such being the main ingredients in larceny, the reader will note that this particular offense has, more than any other known to and originally constituted by our unwritten law, been affected by legislative intervention. Of choses in action (Art. 30) or valuable securities, of deeds relating to land, of wills or records, of things affixed to the freehold, or trees growing upon and so parcel of it, of animals *feræ naturæ* (Art. 198), and some other things, larceny could not at common law have been committed. It could only have been committed of "chattel" property, and to this expression our common law assigned a strict and technical significance which excluded the things specified. Now, however, larceny may be committed of such things in virtue of the statute law.[262]

186. Of crimes involving force, mentioned in the four preceding articles, each is allied to other criminal acts more or less serious in degree.

To felonious homicide an assault, aggravated or slight, is akin. An assault cannot be where there was consent by the person alleged to have been assaulted, and difficulty has been felt in determining what is consent. Recently, upon the facts in evidence, it was observed *per judicem:* "There is no consent, though there is no active dissent," and a conviction was upheld upon this distinction.[263]

With robbery and burglary divers criminal acts are closely connected, respecting which special provisions may be found in the statute book.[264] In part these provisions affix, to offenses long previously recognized, specific penalties, in part they alter the pre-existing law, or reproduce enactments which had force prior to the year 1861, and at all events, out of such composite materials—the common, unwritten law, pre-existent statutes and altogether novel ingredients—they consolidate that department of criminal law which concerns larcenous offenses against the person or dwelling-house.

A mere trespass upon land is not *per se* indictable (Art. 12), though it may be punishable if aimed at the effecting of a certain object, or if accompanied by a particular volition or intent; and where any such act by statute entails penal consequences, the significance of words indicating the quality of the act must be satisfied by proofs before a conviction for it can be had. Recently a court of law was called on to decide whether a trespass had been "willful" within the meaning of an act of Parliament.[265]

Simple larceny may, as we have seen, be included in a crime of greater magnitude, or, as we shall presently see (Art. 190), may with difficulty be distinguishable from one or other of certain criminal acts which do not at common law involve the element of force, actual or constructive. Aggravated larceny may be exemplified by reference to the 67th section of the larceny act (24 & 25 Vict. c. 96), which enacts that "whosoever, being a clerk or servant, or being employed for the purpose or in the capacity of a clerk or servant, shall steal any chattel, money, or valuable security belonging to or in the possession or power of his master or employer," shall be guilty of felony, and for the offense thus defined a punishment is awarded more severe than for simple larceny. The nature of aggravated larceny may further be exemplified by reference to the 69th section of the larceny act, which affixes a punishment to the offense of stealing when committed by one employed in the public service of her majesty, or when committed by the police.

187. Criminal responsibility may be incurred by breach of duty or by omission to perform it.

At a trial for manslaughter, it appeared that the relation of master and servant had subsisted between the prisoner and the deceased, and questions arose: 1st, whether the want of proper nourishment and lodging, which the prisoner had neglected to supply to the deceased, was the cause of death; and 2dly, if so, had there been a duty imposed on the prisoner to supply the deceased with such necessaries? It was held that the duty specified had not been imposed, for the deceased was not shown to have been helplessly in the power of the accused and unable to withdraw from it. A conviction therefore could not be had for the offense charged.[266] It is noteworthy, however, that a statutory provision (24 & 25 Vict. c. 100, s. 26) applies where a person is legally liable as master or mistress to provide for an apprentice or servant necessary food, clothing, or lodging, and "willfully and without lawful excuse" refuses or neglects to provide it. The section applies also where a master "unlawfully and maliciously" does bodily harm to his apprentice or servant, so that his life is endangered or his health is permanently injured. In any such case the party offending is guilty of a misdemeanor.

Again, a strict legal duty is imposed on a father to provide for and protect his child, so that when the child is left in a position of danger of which the father knows, and from which he has full power to remove it, and the father neglects his duty of protection and lets the child remain in danger—this is an exposure and abandonment of it by him punishable by statute.[267]

Once more—an indictment will lie against a municipal corporation who have become bound to repair buildings, banks, and so forth, under letters patent from the crown, for not repairing them—this neglect to perform the legal duty cast upon the defendants being indictable.[268]

From cases such as have been above cited, we deduce that the breach of a duty towards the public, to the evil example of others, or directly damaging to the community, may be indictable.

188. There will not, perhaps, in general, be much difficulty in saying whether an act done negligently be indictable.

Where a workman throws rubbish from a housetop on to a road not much frequented, but in which one passing at the moment thus chances to be killed, the act done was wrong, illegal, evidencing gross negligence, a reckless disregard of others, and such an act, causing homicide, might be felonious. And in general, where an act assumes the form of a nuisance, the test to be applied whether it be indictable, is this: Does the alleged nuisance prejudice the public? or is it merely hurtful to the prosecutor? Numerous decisions are to be found upon this point in our reports.[269] A negligent omission or non-feasance might be so culpable as to evidence malice.[270]

Such being an exemplification of indictable negligence at common law, it may be well to add that under particular statutes it has been variously characterized, or associated with words meant to be construed as akin to it.

Thus by section 34 of the act concerning offenses against the person (24 & 25 Vict. c. 100) "whosoever by any unlawful act, or by any willful omission or neglect, shall endanger or cause to be endangered the safety of any person conveyed or being in or upon a railway," shall be guilty of a misdemeanor. And by sec. 36 of the act concerning malicious injuries to property (24 & 25 Vict. c. 97), "whosoever by any unlawful act, or by any willful omission or neglect, shall obstruct or cause to be obstructed any engine or carriage using any railway," shall also be guilty of a misdemeanor.

Where language such as above quoted is used by the Legislature, we may remark as follows: The word "unlawful" applied to an act excludes the case where there has been just cause or excuse, and where applied to an act *primâ facie* criminal—*ex. gr.*, wounding with a weapon—indicates that the act was done willfully, and under circumstances not affording just cause or excuse for doing it. The word "unlawful" affixes to the act done a wrongful, criminal character. The word "willful" is, of course, used in contradistinction to "accidental." The significance of the expression "willful neglect" might be shown by the case of a carriage driven in a reckless and careless manner, or by the case of a truck being knowingly and heedlessly left upon a line of railway, and so obstructing the traffic along it.

189. Malice is often an ingredient in crime. The doing of a wrongful act intentionally, without just cause or excuse, may be characterized as "malicious."

Malice is express or implied—express malice being evidenced by acts, words, or conduct of the accused person, indicative of ill-will towards another—implied malice being evidenced by proof of the doing of an illegal or wrongful act by the accused, which causes harm to person, property or reputation.

For showing the nature of a malicious act, reference may best be made to the statute book, from which some relevant extracts are below given.

The statute 24 & 25 Vict. c. 100, s. 16, contains these words, indicating and defining a particular felony: "Whosoever shall maliciously send, or directly or indirectly cause to be received, knowing the contents thereof, any letter threatening to murder any person, shall be guilty of felony." No difficulty could here arise as to the proof of malice—the act of sending such a letter must obviously be malicious. There might, however, be a doubt whether the expressions in the letter shown to have been sent or caused to be received by the prosecutor, would amount to a threat to murder, and any such doubt would have to be solved by the jury. Words meant merely to alarm, however wrongly used, could not be held to involve a threat to murder.

Malicious acts being of frequent occurrence, have been specially under the cognizance of our Legislature, and many such acts have been provided for by the statute 24 & 25 Vict. c. 97, some references to which may further exemplify this subject.

Thus, by s. 2, "whosoever shall unlawfully and

maliciously set fire to any dwelling-house, any person being therein, shall be guilty of felony." In an indictment framed under this section, the words "unlawfully and maliciously" would appear: they would be equivalent to "willfully without just cause or excuse," and would be opposed to "accidentally." It would not be necessary on the part of the prosecution to adduce evidence of express malice—for instance, of threats uttered, or words of enmity used against the owner of the house or the person who chanced to be within it. If the act were unlawful the malice would be presumed, and to establish the charge it would suffice to show that the building alleged to have been set on fire was a dwelling-house, that some person was in it at the time of the particular transaction, and that it was set fire to willfully, whence the law would infer that the act was done maliciously, mischievously, without just cause or excuse.

Under the 9th section of the act last cited, whosoever shall unlawfully and maliciously, by the explosion of gunpowder or other explosive substance, destroy or damage the whole or part of a dwelling-house, any person being therein, &c., shall be guilty of felony. The words "unlawfully and maliciously" here used are equivalent to willfully, not by accident, and without just cause or excuse.

Regard being had to the distinction between express and implied malice—between malice manifested by words or deeds, and malice inferred as necessarily accompanying a particular course of conduct, or inherent in it, the Legislature has sometimes thought fit to interpose, with a view to preventing a failure of justice, by declaring and defining the kind of malice at which an enactment points, and indicating the kind of proof of malice which may suffice to support an indictment charging it. Thus by sect. 58 of the above-mentioned act, it is enacted that every punishment and forfeiture imposed by the act on any person maliciously committing an offense within its scope, shall equally be enforced, whether the offense be committed from malice conceived against the owner of the property in respect of which it is committed, or otherwise; so that evidence of express malice, conceived against the owner of the property injured, would, on the part of the prosecution, for an offense under the act, be unnecessary. Bearing this provision in mind, we are able to assign a meaning to the words used in the 51st section of the same statute, viz., " Whosoever shall unlawfully and maliciously commit any damage, injury or spoil to or upon any real or personal property whatsoever, either of a public or private nature, for which no punishment is hereinbefore provided, the damage, injury, or spoil being to an amount exceeding £5, shall be guilty of misdemeanor." The damage under this section must have been done unlawfully, *ex. gr.*, through negligence and without just cause or excuse, in order that the case may fall within its operation, but no evidence of express malice, of personal spite or illwill against the owner of the property damaged, need be shown; the word "maliciously" would be satisfied by showing an intent to injure deducible from the circumstances of the case.

In order to sustain a conviction for one or other of certain offenses, proof may have to be given of a particular intent, in addition to the proof of malice. Thus, in the act which concerns offenses against the person (24 & 25 Vict. c. 100), is contained this provision (s. 30): "Whosoever shall unlawfully and maliciously place near any vessel any gunpowder or other explosive substance, with intent to do bodily injury to any person, shall, whether or not any explosion take place, and whether or not any bodily injury be effected, be guilty of felony." To convict under this statutory provision, proof must be given of the intent, which might be answered by showing that the prisoner could not have been aware, when he did the alleged act, that any person was near to the scene of the explosion, or spot where the attempt to cause it was made.

Again, by sect. 28 of the statute 24 & 25 Vict. c. 97, "whosoever shall unlawfully and maliciously cause water to be conveyed or run into any mine, . . with intent thereby to destroy or damage" it, shall be guilty of felony. In support of an indictment framed upon this section, proof might very likely be forthcoming of express malice; if not, malice might be implied from the doing of an unlawful act. The particular intent, viz., to destroy or damage the mine, might, if not expressly proved, be inferred in virtue of the proposition that a man may be supposed to intend that which is the necessary or natural consequence of his act (Art. 173).

The law relating to malicious injuries directed against the person or property of an individual, as exemplified in foregoing paragraphs, has been elaborately codified by the Legislature, and the course of criminal procedure for publishing libelous and defamatory matter, which is indictable at common law, has been in some measure regulated by statute.[271] Of this latter offense, commonly occurring, mention is here made, inasmuch as malice is involved in it; the slanderous act being deliberately and openly done imports malice, evidences a guilty mind.

190. Fraud often gives a criminal color and complexion to conduct which, without this special attribute, would not be punishable ; a cheat having been described by Lord Holt [272] as "a design to impose on the credulity of others, to induce them to believe a thing which is not true." Such is a popular, rather than technical definition of cheating, yet we may safely infer that, in order to justify a conviction for it, there must be in the matter *sub judice* something discernible of which our criminal law can take hold, as constituting or evidencing fraud. The mere expression of an opinion by A., though acted upon by B., and meant to be so, to his prejudice, would not constitute an indictable fraud. The statement by A. that something will happen *in futuro*, as to which B. may exercise his own judgment and common sense, would not constitute an indictable fraud.

Fraud, as must on a moment's reflection be apparent, presents itself in many dissimilar acts, indictable or summarily punishable: for instance, in perjury, forgery, the uttering or passing of bad coin. Any such act involves a fraudulent intent, and our statute book teems with provisions meant to repress fraud under particular circumstances, which the Legislature has singled out and with perspicacity defined. The catalogue, indeed, of statutory offenses involving fraud is long, and still increases; for when a novel kind of fraud presents itself, Parliament may think fit to interfere and check it by special legislation.[273]

Perhaps the most practically important species of statutory fraud is that indicated by the 88th section of the larceny act (24 & 25 Vict. c. 96), viz., the obtaining of money, goods, or valuable securities by false pretenses. "Whosoever shall, by any false pretense, obtain from any other person any chattel, money, or valuable security, with intent to defraud, shall be guilty of a misdemeanor;" the words "valuable security" being defined in sect. 1 of the act.

This statutory misdemeanor comprises the following ingredients: 1st, a false pretense; 2dly, a making of such pretense with intent to defraud; 3dly, the obtaining thereby of some chattel, money, or valuable security. The main distinction between this misdemeanor and the felony of stealing is that in the latter there must be a taking—theoretically, a forcible taking—whereas in the former the property in the chattel is voluntarily transferred to the defendant (Art. 185).

To exhibit this distinction more at length: Where A., the owner of a chattel, induced by a false statement made by B., transfers to him the chattel, meaning to pass the property in as well as the possession of it, the person guilty of the fraud is not indictable for larceny; but where the owner of the chattel intended to part with the possession of it only, and the person guilty of the fraud obtained such possession only, the result is different. A. may, however, by a trick. get possession of a chattel belonging to B., the property in which is not meant to pass save on performance of a condition which is not performed; in this case a conviction for larceny might be supported if the chattel were appropriated *invito domino*. But if the property in the chattel be meant to pass as well as the possession of it, this surrender or transfer being induced by a trick or false representation, then an indictment for the statutory offense of cheating might be supported. In the former of these cases there is in contemplation of law—whereas in the latter there is not—a larcenous taking of the chattel.[274]

By reason of the somewhat subtle distinctions between the felony of larceny and the misdemeanor of obtaining money by false pretenses, which will be further illustrated in the next chapter, it has been enacted that if upon the trial of any person charged with misdemeanor, the evidence shows that he obtained the property in such manner as to amount in law to larceny, he shall not by reason thereof be entitled to be acquitted of the misdemeanor.[275]

191. For facilitating and rendering more complete the comparison of crime with tort, and having regard to what has been said in Art. 152 as to the doctrine of ratification, and that of finality as connected with wrongful acts, I would add that in criminal procedure ratification assumes the special form of adoption—of guilty knowledge and connivance after an act done. Thus a *feme covert*, in her husband's absence and without his knowledge, received stolen goods and paid money on account of them. The thief and the husband afterwards met, and the husband then learned that the goods were stolen, agreed as to the price for them, and paid the balance to the thief. The husband was held, upon these facts, to have been properly convicted of receiving the goods knowing them to have been stolen.[276]

An accessory after the fact is one who, knowing a felony to have been committed, receives, relieves, comforts, or assists the felon. He in a certain sense may be said to have adopted the criminal act, and *ex post facto* to have connived at it.

Then, as regards the doctrine of finality in connection with criminal procedure, this being technically at suit of the sovereign, the rule of our unwritten law, *tempus non occurrit regi*, generally applies; but upon this rule many inroads have been made by statute in reference both to indictable offenses and to offenses summarily punishable. The drift of modern legislation has clearly been to restrict the time within which a prosecution may be commenced, a summons taken out, or an information laid; and the provisions upon this subject promulgated by the Legislature have been in favor of finality and in prevention of vexatious litigation.

192. Doubtless our criminal law, and the mode of administering it, have been zealously cared for by the Legislature and the judges. Although not absolutely perfect—for what human code or institution is or can be?—criminal law and the administration of it have attained in this country to very great excellence; nor is it the least likely that any changes yet to be made in them will belie the utterances of Parliament and the bench hitherto often made when legislating or adjudicating in a merciful and benignant spirit.

CHAPTER IX.

LEGAL PRINCIPLES APPLIED TO CRIMES.

"Though hand join in hand, the wicked shall not be unpunished."
PROVERBS.

193. NOTWITHSTANDING the above emphatic assurance given by the wisest of men, criminals do occasionally slip through the meshes of the net which law ingeniously spreads, and escape the punishment which might seem due to their misdeeds. Subjoined cases show how this evasion may chance to happen, vindicating nevertheless the astuteness of our legal draftsmen.

---

194. A. having a horse which he knew to be vicious and dangerous, and to have kicked and injured persons, turned it out upon a common on which he had a right of pasture, and through which to his knowledge passed footpaths much frequented by the public, and not fenced off from the common. B., a child about eight years old, whilst on or very near to a pathway—the evidence being doubtful as to this point—across the common, was kicked by the horse and killed.

It was held upon the foregoing facts, that A. had been properly convicted of manslaughter, as having been guilty of culpable negligence causing death. "Turning out a horse upon a common traversed by a public highway, if done with the knowledge that the horse is vicious, is unlawful, and if death ensues from such culpable negligence, the offense of manslaughter is complete."[277]

195. A. was indicted for wounding B. with intent to do him grievous bodily harm, which is a statutory felony. It appeared that A. and B. were in the habit of boating after wild fowl at night in a neighboring river, that A. was jealous of B.'s intrusion on a part of the river which he specially visited, and, when the act investigated was done, fired off his gun in the direction of the prosecutor, not, as seemed, with intent to kill or cause bodily hurt, but rather with the intention of frightening the prosecutor, and so deterring him from again coming into that part of the river after wild fowl.

The jury, negativing the existence of a felonious intent as having actuated the defendant, found nevertheless that he had been guilty of a statutory misdemeanor, that, viz., of unlawfully and maliciously wounding. The intent accordingly laid in the indictment was negatived, though there was evidence that the act which injured the prosecutor was done with *malus animus*, inasmuch as the defendant was not justified in trying to alarm the prosecutor. This case shows, the conviction having been affirmed, that a guilty mind accompanying an act, may give to it the color of malice in the eye of our law.[278]

In a case which recently came before a crown court the defendant was indicted for "unlawfully and maliciously" causing damage to property of the prosecutor. The proofs showed that defendant had thrown a stone at persons in the street, intending to strike one or other of them, but missing them the stone had broken prosecutor's window. The jury expressly negatived the intention to break the window, and the court unanimously held that the defendant could not be convicted of maliciously breaking it. A man could not be said to have maliciously done that which he did not mean to do.[279]

196. In the following case, decided upon facts very different from those just set out, the effect of a course of conduct, which was illegal, in giving color to an act done during its continuance, was also considered with a result favorable to the accused person.

The defendant's business was that of manufacturing fire-works contrary to the statute law (9 & 10 Will. III, c. 7). A fire broke out amongst combustibles in his possession, and being used for the purpose of his business. The fire having ignited a rocket being on the defendant's premises, caused it to fly across the street and set fire to a house opposite, whereby a person's death was occasioned. The defendant was absent at the time of this mishap, which occurred through the negligence of his servants.

A conviction for manslaughter was upon these facts held not sustainable, for "the fire which caused the death did not happen through any personal interference or negligence of the defendant. The keeping of the fire-works in the house was disconnected with the negligence of the defendant's servants," from which the death ensued. [230]

---

197. The prisoner was indicted for stealing a lamb under the following circumstances: it appeared that, having in the first instance put twenty-nine black-faced lambs, belonging to himself, into a field which contained ten white-faced lambs of the prosecutor, he afterwards took away his own lambs and offered them for sale as amounting in number to twenty-nine. The proposed purchaser,

however, on counting the lambs, pointed out to the prisoner that there were in fact thirty in the flock, which included one white-faced lamb belonging to the prosecutor. The prisoner nevertheless sold all the lambs in one lot to the other party on his own individual account. On the trial of this case, the jury found that at the time of leaving the field the prisoner did not know that the prosecutor's lamb was in the flock, but that he had a felonious intention when he sold it. The question accordingly was, could the prisoner, upon the above facts and finding, be convicted of larceny? It was held that he might be so, upon reasoning of this kind: the original taking was wrongful,—for assuming that the prisoner was ignorant of the fact of the lamb being in his flock when he drove it from the field, the so driving it away and keeping it was a tortious act involving a trespass; and this act of continuing trespass became felonious when the prisoner, knowing that the lamb in question was not his own, sold it.[281]

Larceny, we have seen (Art. 185), does at common law include a taking, and the above case is peculiar in so far as the doctrine of relation was applied in it, so as to render the transaction *sub judice* felonious.

198. Simple larceny could at common law be committed of movable or chattel property only, and could only be committed of that which was the subject of property, a doctrine which has led to some curious results and nice distinctions. Let us suppose, for instance, that lead fixed to the dwelling-house of A. was torn off and detached from it and carried away immediately by B., with a felonious intent to appropriate it to his own use. A conviction could not at common law be had against B. for stealing this lead, because it had been affixed to the freehold and so savored of the realty. But if B., having severed the lead one day, came on to the premises the next day and took it away, he might be found guilty of larceny at common law, and the property in the lead, severed and converted into a movable, having become vested in A., as owner of the freehold, would be so laid or described in the indictment against B. for stealing it.

Similarly at common law larceny could not be committed of animals, wild and unreclaimed, as of rabbits in a warren; therefore, if a man wrongfully killed such an animal and carried it away for his own use, he must have been acquitted on an indictment for stealing it, the transaction of killing and carrying away being continuous and indivisible. If, however, there were a decided break in such transaction, the result might be different, inasmuch as larceny could be committed of the flesh of an animal *fera naturæ* which would serve for food. Therefore, if the defendant, having unlawfully killed a rabbit on the prosecutor's land, abandoned and left it there, and after the lapse of some time returned and took it away, he might be convicted of stealing the rabbit.[282]

Statutory provisions are in force which relate to the stealing of lead from a building and to the unlawful killing of rabbits.[283]

---

199. The defendant induced the prosecutor to purchase a chain from him by fraudulently representing that it was of 15-carat gold, whereas in fact it was of a quality little better than 6-carat gold knowing at the time that he was falsely representing the quality of the chain. A conviction for the statutory misdemeanor mentioned in Art. 190, was upon the above facts upheld, for the statement that the chain was of 15-carat gold could not be regarded as mere exaggerated praise, nor as relating to a mere matter of opinion; it was a statement as to a specific fact within defendant's knowledge, and so constituted a false pretense.[251]

The nature of an indictable cheat may be thus
18

further shown: A. ordered goods of B. (the prosecutor), saying that he 'wished to pay ready money for them. A. gave checks for the price of the goods, not however intending to meet them, but meaning to defraud. This was held to amount to a representation by defendant that the checks would be paid—that the existing state of facts was such that in ordinary course they would be met. The giving of a check does not, however, *per se* necessarily imply that the person giving it then has money to the needful amount in the bank upon which the check is drawn; he may intend to pay in money to meet it, or he may be authorized by the banker to overdraw his account.[285] Misapprehension as regards this matter ought no longer to exist.

200. The subjoined statement of facts may throw light upon the component ingredients in the crime of larceny.

The prisoner, being a depositor in a post-office savings bank, presented an order for payment of money sent to the office at which he applied for it by that in which he was a depositor. The warrant for payment being handed to the clerk, a sum much exceeding that specified in it, and much exceeding the amount of prisoner's deposit was, through a mistake handed to him by the clerk. Whereupon the prisoner took up the money and went away, *animo furandi*, and knowing the money not to be his.

Upon these facts, as found by the jury, the prisoner was held to have been guilty of larceny.[256] The main question was: Had there been a taking— a felonious taking, essential to the constitution of simple larceny at common law? (Art. 185 (1)). Now where the true owner of a chattel parted with the physical possession of it to the prisoner, so that in one sense the taking of possession was not against the prosecutor's will, yet if it be proved that the prisoner from the beginning had the intent to steal, and with that intent obtained possession of the thing, there is a sufficient taking of it to satisfy our customary law, and since the taking was with a felonious intent, there was a stealing.

Upon facts such as above stated, a test somewhat differently worded may also be applied for determining the nature and quality of the act done by the accused. Had the property in the money wrongfully obtained passed to the prisoner when he assumed dominion over it, and dealt with it as his own? Not so; the money was technically, as it had before been, the property of the postmaster general, and never vested in the prisoner, the case being similar to that of a person handing to a cabman a sovereign by mistake for a shilling, the property in the sovereign not thus becoming vested in the cabman, and the question whether he was guilty of larceny in appropriating it depending upon whether the cabman at the time he took the sovereign was aware of the mistake, and had then the guilty intent to appropriate it—the *animus furandi.*

201. The distinction between the felony of larceny and the misdemeanor of obtaining goods, money, or a valuable security by false pretenses, may be illustrated by reference to two well-known kinds of agency, a general and a special agency.

Where a servant authorized generally to act for his master in his business is intrusted with his master's property, and being so intrusted is induced by fraud to part with it, the person guilty of the fraud might be convicted of obtaining the property by false pretenses, but would not be guilty of larceny.

Where, however, a servant is intrusted by his master with the possession of goods for a special purpose, and is tricked out of that possession by fraud, the person practicing the fraud is guilty of the crime of larceny.

Now the ground of the distinction is this: in the first of these two cases there would be no evidence of a taking against the will of the owner, the servant having given up the property voluntarily, and meaning to part with it, and his act being the act of his principal.

In the latter case the servant had no authority to part with the property in the goods except to fulfill the special purpose for which they were intrusted to him, and therefore there was no surrendering or giving up of the property by the master through his agent. There was no taking by the prisoner, no ideal element of force in what he did.

Subtle as the above distinction may possibly be deemed, it has sometimes in connection with matters of practical importance come under judicial notice. The cashier of a bank is authorized generally to conduct the business of the bank within his own particular sphere of action, and to part with its property on presentation of a genuine order from a customer, as to the genuineness of which he (the cashier) must judge. If being deceived by a forged order he parts with the money of the bank, he parts with the property in it as well as with the possession of it. There is under such circumstances no evidence of a taking, nothing, therefore, to support an indictment for larceny as against a person obtaining the money by a forged check or order. He might, however, be properly convicted on a charge of obtaining money by false pretenses.[287]

---

202. Magisterial functions are most usefully exercised for the repression and punishment of crime, and this list of cases may therefore fitly terminate with the recital of a peculiar state of facts, relating to the duties of justices, which recently presented itself.

It is an established and fundamental rule of law that a man shall not be twice punished, nor even be twice put in peril, on the same criminal charge, though if from any particular circumstance a trial has proved abortive, the case may then be submitted a second time to the consideration of a jury, and determined as right and justice may require. This rule generally holds irrespective of the degree or quality of the offense charged, the test by which to determine its applicability being this: Was the accused person really in jeopardy at his first trial? The mere statement of this test shows how the rule must be understood, and subject to what qualifications it must be received, for cases occur in which a judge may properly in the exercise of his discretion discharge a jury without giving a verdict, as where a juryman, or the prisoner, or the judge himself has been taken ill, and so the trial has been abruptly terminated, or where the jury are unable to agree.

Involving an apparent applicability of the above rule, a question arose of this nature: Under certain statutory regulations, a charge of assault may be heard and adjudicated on by justices of the peace, and if at the hearing the complaint is dismissed upon the merits, or as too trifling to deserve punishment, the justices are required to give to the defendant a certificate stating the fact of such dismissal, and by stat. 24 & 25 Vict. c. 100, s. 45, the obtaining of such certificate, or conviction with payment of the fine or undergoing the imprisonment awarded, shall operate as a release from all other proceedings, civil or criminal, for the same cause. Does then a conviction for an assault by justices at petty sessions at the instance of the person assaulted, and imprisonment in pursuance of such conviction, bar an indictment subsequently preferred against the same defendant for manslaughter, the person assaulted having died from the effects of the assault? It was held that the proceeding by indictment was not thus barred, the short ground of this decision being that the statutory provision applies only where there has been a former judicial decision on the same accusation, and where the question in dispute has so been previously adjudged. The charge of assault was not the same as that of manslaughter,[288] and accordingly the principle adverted to at the commencement of this article has not by the decision given been infringed.

203. I must now take leave of the reader of this little volume, and in doing so what am I to say? I express a hope that a perusal of its pages will show that the study of English law is not so encumbered by technicalities as may have been supposed, that knowledge of it is quite accessible to every educated man—is, indeed, easily within his grasp—and that a position involving difficulties and anxiety may often be avoided by prudent foresight and the exercise of common sense strengthened and tutored by some familiarity with legal science.

CASES, ETC., REFERRED TO.

1. *Per* Willes, J., Lee *v.* Bude and Torrington Junction R. C., L. R. 6 C. P. 576, 582.
2. The Stourbridge Union *v.* The Droitwich Union, L. R. 6 Q. B. 769.
3. Godsall *v.* Boldero, 9 East, 72.
4. Dalby *v.* The India and London Life Assurance Co., 15 C. B. 365.
5. Lord Mansfield's Decisions by Evans, p. iv.
6. *Vide per* North, C. J., Barnardiston *v.* Soame, 6 Howell, State Tri. 1094, 1095.
7. *Vide per* Lord Brougham, O'Connell *v.* Reg., 11 Cl. & F. 328.
8. See Blackhouse *v.* Bonomi, 9 H. L. Cas. 503.
9. Smith *v.* London and St. Catharine's Docks Co., L. R. 3 C. P. 326, with which compare Collis *v.* Selden, Id. 495.
10. Chandelor *v.* Lopus, Cro. Jac. 2.
11. Reg. *v.* Ardley, L. R. 1 C. C. 301.
12. Reg. *v.* Gurney, rep. by Finlason, pp. 215, 216.
13. *Ex parte* Wason, L. R. 4 Q. B. 573.
14. Benjamin *v.* Storr, L. R. 9 C. P. 400.
15. Farrant *v.* Barnes, 11 C. B. N. S. 553; Brass *v.* Maitland, 6 E. & B. 470.
16. Williams *v.* East India Co., 3 East, 192.

17. Penruddock's Case, 5 Rep. 100; Jones v. Williams, 11 M. & W. 176.
18. Burridge v. Nicholetts, 6 H. & N. 383.
19. Blades v. Higgs, 11 H. L. Cas. 621, with which compare Chambers v. Miller, 13 C. B. N. S. 125; Smith v. Wright, 6 H. & N. 821.
20. Mortimore v. Wright, 6 M. & W. 482. See also Ruttinger v. Temple, 4 B. & S. 491.
21. See, for instance, Shadwell v. Shadwell, 9 C. B. N. S. 159; Begbie v. Phosphate Sewage Co., L. R. 10 Q. B. 491.
22. Forth v. Stanton, 1 Saund. 210.
23. *Per* Cockburn, C. J., Callisher v. Bischoffsheim, L. R. 5 Q. B. 449.
24. Kendal v. Wood, L. R. 6 Ex. 243; Newall v. Tomlinson, L. R. 6 C. P. 405; Freeman v. Jeffries, L. R. 4 Ex. 189, 197.
25. Kennedy v. Broun, 13 C. B. N. S. 677.
26. Martin v. Great Indian Peninsular Railway Co., L. R. 3 Ex. 9.
27. Burrows v. Marsh Gas and Coke Co., L. R. 7 Ex. 96; 5 Id. 67.
28. Helps v. Clayton, 17 C. B. N. S. 553.
29. See Stats. 30 & 31 Vict. c. 144; 31 & 32 Vict. c. 86.
30. Stokes v. Lewis, 1 l. R. 20.
31. Stanley v. Dowdeswell, L. R. 10 C. P. 102.
32. Johnston v. Sumner, 3 H. & N. 261.
33. Stat. 33 & 34 Vict. c. 93.
34. See Stat. 37 & 38 Vict. c. 62.
35. Melhado v. Porto Alegre Railway Co., L. R. 9 C. P. 503.
36. Kelner v. Baxter, L. R. 2 C. P. 174.
37. Ashbury Railway Carriage Company v. Riche, H. L. June 8, 1875, reported 44 Law Jour. Ex. 184.
38. Brook v. Hook, L. R. 6 Ex. 89.
39. Stubbs v. Holywell Railway Co., L. R. 2 Ex. 311.
40. Robinson v. Davison, L. R. 6 Ex. 269.
41. Farrow v. Wilson, L. R. 4 C. P. 744.

42. Prestwich v. Poley, 18 C. B. N. S. 806; Strauss v. Francis, L. R. 1 Q. B. 379.
43. Lovegrove v. White, L. R. 6 C. P. 440.
44. Per Lord Chelmsford, Couston v. Chapman, L. R. 2 Sc. App. 254.
45. Id. 256.
46. Judgment, Appleby v. Meyers, L. R. 1 C. P. 615; s. c. 2 Id. 651.
47. Vide per Byles, J., Keene v. Beard, 8 C. B. N. S. 372.
48. Roper v. Johnson, L. R. 8 C. P. 167.
49. Frost v. Knight, L. R. 7 Ex. 111.
50. Hall v. Wright, E. B. & E. 746; Beechey v. Brown, Id. 796.
51. Hadley v. Baxendale, 9 Exch. 341; Horne v. Midland Railway Co., L. R. 8 C. P. 131, 140.
52. Hobbs v. London & Southwestern Railway Co., L. R. 10 Q. B. 111.
53. Per Bovill, C. J., Woodyer v. Great Western Railway Co., L. R. 2 C. P. 318.
54. Kemble v. Farren, 6 Bing. 141; Magee v. Lavell, L. R. 9 C. P. 107, 115.
55. Per Lord Romilly. Spackman v. Evans, L. R. 3 H. L. 239.
56. Per Lord Cairns, Reese River Silver Mining Co. v. Smith, 4 H. L. 79, 80.
57. Per Lord Hatherley, C., Id. 73.
58. Thoroughgood's Case, 2 Rep. 9 b.
59. Foster v. Mackinnon, L. R. 4 C. P. 704.
60. Kennedy v. Panama &c. Mail Co., L. R. 2 Q. B. 580, 587.
61. Cowan v. Milbourn, L. R. 2 Ex. 230.
62. Begbie v. Phosphate Sewage Co., L. R. 10 Q. B. 491.
63. Burton v. Pinkerton, L. R. 2 Ex. 340.
64. Per Wilmot, C. J., Collins v. Blantern, 2 Wilson R. 341.
65. Mitchel v. Reynolds, 1 P. Williams, 181.
66. Bolton v. Madden, L. R. 9 Q. B. 55.
67. Richardson v. Williamson, L. R. 6 Q. B. 276, 279.
68. Vide per Keating, J., Turner v. Goulden, L. R. 9 C. P. 58.
69. Turner v. Mason, 14 M. & W. 112.

70. Harmer v. Cornelius, 5 C. B. N. S. 236.
71. See Couturier v. Hastie, 5 H. L. Cas. 673.
72. Lamert v. Heath, 15 M. & W. 486.
73. Smidt v. Tiden, L. R. 9 Q. B. 446.
74. Great Northern Railway Co. v. Witham, L. R. 9 C. P. 16.
75. Borries v. Imperial Ottoman Bank, L. R. 9 C. P. 38.
76. Armstrong v. Stodes, L. R. 7 Q. B. 598.
77. Hutton v. Bulloch, L. R. 9 Q. B. 572.
78. Abbott on Shipping, 11th ed. 195.
79. Ford v. Cotesworth, L. R. 5 Q. B. 544; see also Ashcroft v. Crow Orchard Colliery Co., L. R. 9 Q. B. 540.
80. Judgment, Hale v. Rawson, 4 C. B. N. S. 95.
81. Howell v. Coupland, L. R. 9 Q. B. 462; s. c. affirmed Jan. 18, 1876.
82. Bloomer v. Bernstein, L. R. 9 C. P. 588; with which compare Freeth v. Burr, Id. 208; Morgan v. Bain, L. R. 10 C. P. 15.
83. Shepherd v. Harrison, L. R. 5 H. L. 116.
84. City Discount Co. v. McLean, L. R. 9 C. P. 692.
85. Thorn v. Mayor &c. of London, L. R. 9 Ex. 163; s. c. affi'd 44 L. J. Ex. 63, and in H. L. February 18, 1876.
86. Gunn v. Roberts, L. R. 9 C. P. 331.
87. Stephens v. Australian Insurance Co., L. R. 8 C. P. 18.
88. Goodwin v. Robarts, L. R. 10 Ex. 353.
89. Ashforth v. Bedford, L. R. 9 C. P. 20.
90. Petrocochino v. Bott, L. R. 9 C. P. 355.
91. Bartonshill Coal Co. v. Reid, 3 Macq. Sc. App. Cas. 266.
92. Morgan v. Vale of Neath Railway Co., L. R. 1 Q. B. 149.
93. Murray v. Currie, L. R. 6 C. P. 24.
94. Stewart v. West India & Pacific Steamship Co., L. R. 8 Q. B. 88.
95. Heywood v. Pickering, L. R. 9 Q. B. 428.
96. Head v. Tattersall, L. R. 7 Ex. 7.
97. Judgment, Nugent v. Smith, 45 Law Journ. 28.
98. Smith v. Hughes, L. R. 6 Q. B. 597.
99. Ionides v. Pender, L. R. 9 Q. B. 531, 537.

100. M'Gowan v. Dyer, L. R. 8 Q. B. 141.
101. Udell v. Atherton, 7 H. & N. 172.
102. Blair v. Bromley, 2 Phillips, 354.
103. Fivaz v. Nicholls, 2 C. B. 501.
104. Williams v. Bayley, L. R. 1 H. L. 200.
105. Taylor v. Chester, L. R. 4 Q. B. 309.
106. Waugh v. Morris, L. R. 8 Q. B. 202.
107. Ramsden v. Lupton, L. R. 9 Q. B. 17.
108. Dudgeon v. Pembroke, L. R. 9 Q. B. 581; see s. c. L. R. 1 Q. B. D. 96.
109. Fenwick v. Brinkworth, 2 Foster & Finlason, 86; Pym v. Campbell, 6 E. & B. 370, 374.
110. Ireland v. Livingston, L. R. 5 H. L. 395, 416.
111. *Per* Skynner, C. B., Rann v. Hughes, 7 T. R. 350 (*a*).
112. Peirce v. Corf, L. R. 9 Q. B. 210.
113. Stat. 19 & 20 Vict. c. 97, s. 3.
114. *Vide per* Parke, B., Kennaway v. Treleavan, 5 M. & W. 501.
115. Batard v. Hawes, 2 E. & B. 289.
116. Mountstephen v. Lakeman, L. R. 7 Q. B. 196.
117. *Per* Bovill, C. J., Coles v. Pack, L. R. 5 C. P. 70; Nottingham Hide Co. v. Bottrill, L. R. 8 C. P. 694.
118. Lee v. Jones, 17 C. B. N. S. 482; Railton v. Matthews, 10 Cl. & F. 934.
119. Crago v. Jones, L. R. 8 Ex. 78, 82.
120. Phillips v. Foxall, L. R. 7 Q. B. 166.
121. Davidson v. Cooper, 13 M. & W. 343.
122. Swift v. Jewsbury, L. R. 9 Q. B. 301; Barwick v. English Joint Stock Bank, L. R. 2 Ex. 259.
123. Heilbutt v. Hickson, L. R. 7 C. P. 438, 449.
124. Martineau v. Kitching, L. R. 7 Q. B. 436.
125. Holmes v. Hoskins, 9 Ex. 753.
126. Beaumont v. Brengeri, 5 C. B. 301; see also Marshall v. Green, L. R. 1 C. P. D. 35.
127. Sharman v. Brandt, L. R. 6 Q. B. 720.
128. Mews v. Carr, 1 H. & N. 484.
129. See Sievewright v. Archibald, 17 Q. B. 103.

130. Stewart v. Eddowes, L. R. 9 C. P. 311.
131. Per Best, C. J., Wells v. Horton, 4 Bing. 43.
132. Knowlmann v. Blewett, L. R. 9 Ex. 307.
133. Chasemore v. Turner, L. R. 10 Q. B. 500.
134. Co. Lit. 35 b.
135. Perkins, Prof. Book, Chap. II, s. 117.
136. Bla. Com. Vol. II, Chap. 20. In re Sandilands, L. R. 6 Q. B. 411; Xenos v. Wickham, L. R. 2 H. L. 312.
137. Noy, Max. 9th ed. p. 24.
138. Webb v. Herne Bay Commissioners, L. R. 5 Q. B. 642.
139. Trevivan v. Lawrence, 1 Salk. 276.
140. Shower v. Pilck, 4 Ex. 478.
141. Marchant v. Lee Conservancy Board, L. R. 8 Ex. 290; Austin v. Guardians of St. Matthew, Bethnal Green, 43 L. J. C. P. 100.
142. Mayor of Berwick v. Oswald, 5 H. L. Cas. 856.
143. Nedham's Case, 8 Rep. 135 a.
144. Laughter's Case, 5 Rep. 22.
145. Brown v. Corporation of London, 13 C. B. N. S. 828.
146. Litt. s. 335, note by Hargrave and Butler.
147. Vynior's Case, 8 Rep. 81.
148. Collins v. Blantern, 2 Wils. 341.
149. Mitchel v. Reynolds, 1 P. Wms. 181.
150. Per Parke, B., Great Northern Railway Co. v. Harrison, 12 C. B. 609.
151. Barrett v. Duke of Bedford, 8 T. R. 602, 605.
152. Charlesworth v. Holt, L. R. 9 Ex. 38.
153. Pordage v. Cole, 1 Saund. 319; Cutler v. Bower, 11 Q. B. 973.
154. Compare Marquis of Bute v. Thompson, 13 M. & W. 487; Lord Clifford v. Watts, L. R. 5 C. P. 577.
155. Reid v. Hoskins, 6 E. & B. 953; Avery v. Bowden, Id. 962.
156. Sanderson v. Aston, L. R. 8 Ex. 73.
157. Harrison v. Seymour, L. R. 1 C. P. 518.
158. Hill v. Foley, 2 H. L. Cas. 28; Pott v. Clegg, 16 M. & W. 321.

159. *Vide per* Bayley, J., Hall *v.* Fuller, 5 B. & C. 750; Young *v.* Grote, 4 Bing. 253; *per* Maule, J., Robarts *v.* Tucker, 16 Q. B. 577.
160. 24 & 25 Vict. c. 98, ss. 23-25, 38.
161. British Linen Co. *v.* Caledonian Insurance Co., 4 Macq. Sc. App. Cas. 107.
162. Fowkes *v.* The Manchester and London Life Assurance and Loan Association, 3 B. & S. 917.
163. Macdonald *v.* Law Union Fire and Life Insurance Co., L. R. 9 Q. B. 328.
164. *Vide per Judicem*, L. R. 6 Ex. 144.
165. Jackson *v.* Union Marine Insurance Co., L. R. 10 C. P. 125.
166. Denton *v.* Great Northern Railway Co., 5 E. & B. 860; Readhead *v.* Midland Railway Co., L. R. 4 Q. B. 379.
167. Hurst *v.* Great Western Railway Co., 19 C. B. N. S. 310.
168. See Bridges *v.* North London Railway Co., L. R. 7 H. L. 213.
169. Ellis *v.* Great Western Railway Co., L. R. 9 C. P. 551.
170. *Vide per curiam* Great Northern Railway Co. *v.* Harrison, 10 Exch. 376.
171. M'Cawley *v.* Furness Railway Co., L. R. 8 Q. B. 57.
172. Gallin *v.* London and Northwestern Railway Co., L. R. 10 Q. B. 212.
173. Belfast and Ballymena Railway Co. *v.* Keys, 9 H. L. Cas. 556.
174. Bailiff Jurats of Romney Marsh *v.* Corporation of the Trinity House, L. R. 7 Ex. 247; with which compare Holmes *v.* Mather, L. R. 10 Ex. 261.
175. Dennis, app., Tovell, resp., L. R. 8 Q. B. 10.
176. Armory *v.* Delamirie, 1 Stra. 504.
177. Halliday *v.* Holgate, L. R. 3 Ex. 299.
178. Hall *v.* Pickard, 3 Camp. 187.
179. Lotan *v.* Cross, 2 Camp. 464.
180. Lord *v.* Price, L. R. 9 Ex. 54.
181. Pickering *v.* James, L. R. 8 C. P. 489.
182. Clementson *v.* Mason, L. R. 10 C. P. 209.
183. *Per* Lord Holt, Ashby *v.* White, 2 Ld. Raym. 9, 55.

184. Atkinson v. Newcastle and Gateshead Waterworks Co., L. R. 6 Ex. 404.
185. Winch v. Conservators of the Thames, L. R. 9 C. P. 378.
186. Smith v. Darby, L. R. 7 Q. B. 716, 722; Eadon v. Jeffcock, L. R. 7 Ex. 379.
187. Dunn v. Birmingham Canal Co., 42 L. J. Q. B. 34.
188. Baird v. Williamson, 15 C. B. N. S. 376.
189. Compare Fletcher v. Rylands, L. R. 3 H. L. 330; Smith v. Fletcher, L. R. 9 Ex. 64.
190. Nield v. London and Northwestern Railway Co., L. R. 10 Ex. 4.
191. Holker v. Porritt, L. R. 10 Ex. 59.
192. Oliver v. Northeastern Railway Co., L. R. 9 Q. B. 409.
193. Booth v. Wilson, 1 B. & Ald. 59.
194. Hadley v. Taylor, L. R. 1 C. P. 53.
195. John v. Bacon, L. R. 5 C. P. 437.
196. See, for instance, Gwinnell v. Eamer, L. R. 10 C. P. 658.
197. Baldwin v. Casella, L. R. 7 Ex. 325; Appleby v. Percy, L. R. 9 C. P. 647.
198. May v. Burdett, 9 Q. B. 101; Jackson v. Smithson, 15 M. & W. 563.
199. Northeastern Railway Co. v. Wanless, L. R. 7 H. L. 12; Bridges v. North London Railway Co., Id. 213; Jackson v. Metropolitan Railway Co., L. R. 10 C. P. 49.
200. Per Wightman, J., Tuff v. Warman, 5 C. B. N. S. 585; Radley v. London and Northwestern Railway Co., L. R. 2 Ex. 71.
201. Waite v. Northeastern Railway Co., E. B. & E. 719.
202. Child v. Hearn, L. R. 9 Ex. 176.
203. Thorogood v. Binyan, 8 C. B. 115.
204. Arsmstrong v. Lancashire and Yorkshire Railway Co., L. R. 10 Ex. 47.
205. Moriarty v. London, Chatham and Dover Railway Co., L. R. 5 Q. B. 314, 319.
206. Read v. Great Eastern Railway Co., L. R. 3 Q. B. 555.
207. Dawson v. Midland Railway Co., L. R. 8 Ex. 8.
208. Calye's Case, 8 Co. Rep. 32.

209. Cashill v. Wright, 6 E. & B. 891, 900.
210. Burgess v. Clements, 4 M. & S. 306, 310, 311.
211. Morgan v. Ravey, 6 H. & N. 265, 277.
212. Dawson v. Chamney, 5 Q. B. 164.
213. Western Counties Manure Co. v. Lawes Chemical Manure Co., L. R. 9 Ex. 218, 222.
214. Wren v. Wield, L. R. 4 Q. B. 730.
215. Redway v. McAndrew, L. R. 9 Q. B. 74.
216. Johnson v. Emerson, L. R. 6 Ex. 329, 372.
217. Miller v. David, L. R. 9 C. P. 118; Dickeson v. Hilliard, L. R. 9 Ex. 79.
218. Hunt v. Goodlake, 43 L. J. C. P. 54.
219. Judgment, Cooke v. Wildes, 5 E. & B. 340; Taylor v. Hawkins, 16 Q. B. 308; Dawkins v. Lord Rokeby, L. R. 8 Q. B. 255; Laughton v. Bishop of Sodor and Man, L. R. 4 P. C. 495, 502.
220. Stat. 6 & 7 Vict. c. 96.
221. Falvey v. Stanford, L. R. 10 Q. B. 54.
222. Gerhard v. Bates, 2 E. & B. 476.
223. See, for instance, Small v. Attwood, 6 Cl. & F. 232.
224. Per Bovill, C. J., Ainsworth v. Creeke, L. R. 4 C. P. 475, 486.
225. Brinsmead v. Harrison, L. R. 7 C. P. 547.
226. Judgment, Thomas v. The Queen, L. R. 10 Q. B. 31, 42.
227. Smith v. Cook, L. R. 1 Q. B. D. 79.
228. Foster v. Essex Bank, 17 Mass. Rep. 478; Giblin v. McMullen, L. R. 2 P. C. 317.
229. Lawrence v. Jenkins, L. R. 8 Q. B. 274.
230. See, for instance, Macarthy v. Young, 6 H. & N. 329, 336.
231. Fowler v. Lock, L. R. 10 C. P. 90.
232. See Hartop v. Hoare, 3 Atk. 44; 1 Wils. 8.
233. Wells v. Abrahams, L. R. 7 Q. B. 554.
234. Osborn v. Gillett, L. R. 8 Ex. 88.
235. Bridges, app., Hawkesworth, resp., 21 Law Journ. Q. B. 75.
236. Merry v. Green, 7 M. & W. 623.
237. Catell v. Ireson, E. B. & E. 91.

238. Rex v. Higgins, 2 East, 5; Rex v. Collingwood, 6 Mod. 289.
239. Per Lord Wensleydale, Cooper v. Slade, 6 H. L. Cas. 793.
240. Dickinson v. Fletcher, L. R. 9 C. P. 1.
241. Metcalfe v. London and Brighton Railway Co., 4 C. B. N. S. 307.
242. Vaughton v. London and Northwestern Railway Co., L. R. Ex. 93.
243. Reg. v. Francis, L. R. 2 C. C. R. 128, 132, 133.
244. Nichols v. Hall, L. R. 8 C. P. 322; Reg. v. Hardy, L. R. 1 C. C. R. 278.
245. Reg. v. Daniell, 6 Mod. 99; Cox v. Muncey, 6 C. B. N. S. 375.
246. Reg. v. Sharman, Dearsl. 285.
247. Reg. v. Sharpe, Dearsl. & B. 160.
248. Fitzpatrick v. Kelly, L. R. 8 Q. B. 337.
249. Archb. Cr. Pl. 17th ed. 208, 217.
250. Vide per Blackburn, J., Haigh v. Town Council of Sheffield, L. R. 10 Q. B. 107.
251. Steele v. Brannan, L. R. 7 C. P. 261.
252. Core, app., James, resp., L. R. 1 C. C. 135.
253. Nichols v. Hall, L. R. 8 C. P. 322.
254. R. v. Hickman, 1 Leach Cr. Cas. 278.
255. Crown Law, 128.
256. Stat. 24 & 25 Vict. c. 96, s. 41.
257. 3 Inst. 63.
258. Stat. 24 & 25 Vict. c. 96, s. 58.
259. R. v. Haines, Russ. & Ry. 451; R. v. Hyams, 7 C. & P. 441.
260. Reg. v. M'Kale, L. R. 1 C. C. 125.
261. Reg. v. Jackson, 9 Cox C. Cas. 505.
262. See Stat. 24 & 25 Vict. c. 96, ss. 10–39, and s. 74.
263. Reg. v. Lock, L. R. 2 C. C. R. 10, 14; see Reg. v. Barratt, Id. 81.
264. See Stat. 24 & 25 Vict. c. 96, ss. 40–43, 51 et seq.
265. Foulger v. Steadman, L. R. 8 Q. B. 65.
266. Reg. v. Smith, L. & C. 607.

267. 24 & 25 Vict. c. 100, s. 27; Reg. v. White, L. R. 1 C. C. 311.
268. Mayor and Burgesses of Lyme Regis v. Henley, 2 Cl. & F. 331.
269. See Reg. v. Stevens, L. R. 1 Q. B. 702.
270. Reg. v. Hughes, Dearsl. & B. 248.
271. See Stat. 6 & 7 Vict. c. 96; 32 Geo. III, c. 60.
272. Reg. v. Hathaway, 14 Howell St. Tr. 639.
273. See, for instance, Stat. 37 & 38 Vict. c. 36.
274. Reg. v. Cohen, 2 Den. C. C. 249.
275. Stat. 24 & 25 Vict. c. 96, s. 88.
276. Reg. v. Woodward, L. & C. 122.
277. Reg. v. Dant, L. & C. 567, 574.
278. Reg. v. Ward, L. R. 1 C. C. 356.
279. Reg. v. Pembliton, L. R. 2 C. C. 119.
280. Reg. v. Bennett, Bell C. C. 1.
281. Reg. v. Riley, Dearsl. 149.
282. Reg. v. Townley, L. R. 1 C. C. 315.
283. Stat. 24 & 25 Vict. c. 96, ss. 17, 31.
284. Reg. v. Ardley, L. R. 1 C. C. 301.
285. Reg. v. Hazelton, L. R. 2 C. C. 134.
286. Reg. v. Middleton, L. R. 2 C. C. 38.
287. Reg. v. Prince, L. R. 1 C. C. 150.
288. Reg. v. Morris, L. R. 1 C. C. 90.

INDEX.

ABATEMENT
> of nuisance, what it is, 33.
> is sometimes allowed, 34.

ABSOLUTE AND QUALIFIED RIGHTS,
> distinction between, 164.

ACCEPTANCE OF GOODS
> within statute of frauds, 110.

ACCESSORY
> before the fact, 217.
> after the fact, 265.

ACKNOWLEDGMENT OF DEBT
> to bar the statute of limitations, 118, 119.

ACT OF GOD,
> meaning of this phrase, 88.
> may exonerate innkeeper from liability, 182.

ACT OF PARLIAMENT. *See* STATUTE.

ACTION
> for trespass to land, 25, 154.
> for breach of promise to marry, 55.
> against carrier for loss of goods, 57.
>> delay in transit, 58.
> on contract of suretyship, 101, 134.
> on policy of life insurance, 139.
> on contract, performance of which becomes impossible, 76, 130, 142.
> against railway company for loss of train, 146.
>> a personal hurt, 147.
> for infringement of copyright, &c., 156.
> death caused by negligence, 173–178.
> defamation, 189.

ACTION—*continued.*
>for fraud producing damage, 192-194.
>>negligence in keeping a bull, 198.
>>loss of money deposited at bank, 201.
>>damage to cattle through non-repair of fences, 202.
>>bodily hurt caused by an unruly horse, 204.
>>misappropriating jewels, 208.

AGREEMENT
>is equivalent to contract, 36.
>not to be performed within a year, 117.

AMBIGUOUS CONTRACT,
>how to be interpreted, 85.

ANIMALS FERÆ NATURÆ,
>larceny of, cannot be committed at common law, 250, 272.

ANIMUS FURANDI
>is an ingredient in larceny, 247, 248.

APPELLATE TRIBUNALS.
>their functions, 22.

ASSAULT
>is sometimes permitted by the law, 34.
>cannot be where there is consent, 251.

ASSIGNMENT OF RIGHT OF ACTION
>forbidden at common law, 42.
>exceptions to this rule, 42.

AUCTIONEER,
>how he binds the purchase of property by his signature, 113.

BAILMENT,
>nature of this contract, 184 *et seq.*

BANK,
>misrepresentation by manager of, 108.

BANK NOTES,
>right to by finder of, 210.

BANKERS,
>usage of as regards payment of check, 86.

BILL OF EXCHANGE,
 liability for indorsing it, 60.
   when fraud is practiced, 61.
BILL OF LADING,
 what it is, 78.
 case as to, 78.
 how construed by usage, 83.
BOND,
 what it is, 123.
 how discharged, 124 *et seq*.
BREACH OF DUTY,
 significance of this phrase, 159.
 instances of, actionable, 159 *et seq*.
 in not taking care of animal, 168.
 criminal liability incurred by, 253, 254.
BURGLARY,
 how defined, 240.
 indictment for, 240 *et seq*.

CAPTAIN OF SHIP,
 his authority under certain circumstances, 80.
CARRIER,
 liability of, for loss of goods, 57.
   delay in sending, 58.
 evidence against in action for loss of goods, 218.
CARRIER AND CUSTOMER,
 respective duties of, 31.
CASES DECIDED IN COURTS OF LAW,
 their authority, 20, 22.
CHARTER-PARTY,
 what it is, 75.
 implied contract in, 76, 145.
CHEATING,
 instances of, 224.
 how defined, 262.
 statutable misdemeanor of, 263.
 in selling gold chain, 273.
 in giving check, 274.

CHECK,
> indorsement of, its nature, 51.
> effect of payment by, 86.
> case of paying a forged, considered, 136.

CHOSE IN ACTION,
> what it is, 42.
> is not assignable, 42.
> exceptions to this rule, 42.

CIVIL PROCEDURE
> is ancillary to the asserting of private rights, 25 *et seq*.

COMMON LAW,
> from what sources it has been derived, 18.
> is added to by statutory provisions, 18.
> how enunciated, 20.
> the province of, 24.

CONSENT
> is essential to a contract, 35, 40.
> state of facts illustrating this, 43, 44, 72.

CONSIDERATION
> is an ingredient in a simple contract, 36.
>> essential to its constitution, 37.
> for contract in restraint of trade, 66.
> in mercantile contract exemplified, 68, 71.
> failure of, exemplified, 71.

CONSPIRACY,
> what it is, 30.

CONTRACT. *See* MERCANTILE CONTRACT; WRITTEN INSTRUMENTS.
> meaning of, explained, 35.
> its ingredients, 36, 40.
> ratification of, 46.
> by promoters of a joint stock company, 46.
> *extra vires* cannot be ratified, 47.
> express or implied, what, 48.
> rescission of, when allowed, 52, 55, 61, 71, 77, 78, 88.
> for work and labor, its nature, 54.
> damages recoverable for breach of, 56 *et seq.*, 58.

CONTRACT—*continued.*
>how vitiated by fraud, 60.
>>illegality, 62, 92-95.
>
>may be void as opposed to public policy, 65.
>in restraint of trade, 65.
>the question what it is, answered, 66.
>when performance of, is impossible, 77, 143.

CORPORATION
>must in general contract by deed, 122.

COVENANT,
>what it is, 127.
>how construed, 128 *et seq.*

CRIME,
>its general characteristics, 23, 28, 29, 31, 214 *et seq.*, 221.

CRIMINAL ACT,
>what it is, 214, 220.
>evidence of, 216.
>concerns the public, 221.
>prejudices the public, 221.
>the intent as an ingredient in, 222, 223 *et seq.*
>guilty knowledge as an ingredient in, 227 *et seq.*
>guilty possession as an ingredient in, 228 *et seq.*
>>felonious homicide, 234.
>>robbery, 236.
>>burglary, 239.
>>larceny, 244, 245.
>
>may be constituted by breach of duty, 253.
>>negligence in doing it, 254, 255.
>>maliciously doing it, 256 *et seq.*
>
>may be indictable if involving fraud, 262.

CRIMINAL PROCEDURE,
>what it aims at insuring, 25 *et seq.*

CROWN LAW,
>importance of knowledge of, 213.

DAMAGES,
>what may be given for breach of contract, 55 *et seq.*, 58.

DAMAGES—*continued.*
    in respect to death caused by negligence, 173 *et seq.*
    in an action for defamation, 191.
    for bodily hurt to plaintiff's servant, 208.

DEED,
    how defined, 121.
    its peculiar efficacy, 120, 121.
    evidence in regard to, 121.
    when indispensable, 122.
    different kinds of, 123 *et seq.*
        a bond, 124–127.
        a covenant, 127 *et seq.*

DOCK COMPANY,
    a duty which may be imposed on them, 27.

DURESS,
    contract may be avoided by, 45.

DUTY,
    the nature of a private, 27 *et seq.*

ESTOPPEL,
    by deed, what it is, 120.

EVIDENCE
    of contract, when it must be in writing, 96 *et seq.*
    of negligence, 140, 170–174, 179.
        in action against innkeeper, 179 *et seq.*
    in action for defamation, 190.
        fraud causing damage, 194.
    in special cases founded upon tort, 198 *et seq.*
    verbal or written contract, 98, 101.
    in criminal procedure, 215, 218.
    of criminal intention, 225 *et seq.*
    of guilty knowledge, 227, 231.
    of guilty possession, 228–230, 233.
    on prosecution for felonious homicide, 234–236.
    on a charge of robbery, 237, 239.
    on a prosecution for burglary, 242, 243.
    on a charge of larceny, 249.

FALSE PRETENSES. *See* CHEATING; LARCENY.
FELONY,
    merger of right of action in, 207.
    presumption in favor of married woman accused of, 247.
                infant accused of, 247.
FINALITY
    in litigation is aimed at, 118.
    in action for tort, 196.
    doctrine of, in criminal procedure, 265, 266.
FINDER OF LOST PROPERTY,
    his right to it, 210.
FORBEARANCE TO SUE
    may be a consideration for promise, 38.
FORGERY
    of name to promissory note, its effect, 48.
            check, its effect, 136.
FRAUD. *See* CHEATING.
    directed against an individual, 27.
            the public, 28.
    distinction between public and private, 28–30.
    definition of, 59.
    effect of on contract, 59.
    why evidence is admissible of, 64.
    liability of principal for fraud of agent, 89.
    distinction between moral and legal, 90.
    effect of, in effecting policy of insurance, 139.
    in the formation of a company, 192.
    how, often established at Nisi Prius, 194.
    may render an act indictable, 262.
FRAUDS. *See* STATUTE OF.

GOODS,
    liability of carrier for loss of, 57.
    action for detention of, 154.
    liability of innkeeper for loss of, 179 *et seq*.
    malice in disparaging, 187.
    right of finder to, 210.

GUARANTY,
 nature of it, 75, 103.
 relation between the parties to, 101–104.
 is it continuing or limited as regards time? 105.
 good faith must be observed in, 106.
 effect of alteration of conditions of suretyship, 106, 107, 135.

GUILTY KNOWLEDGE
 may be an ingredient in crime, 222, 228.
 evidence of, 231.

GUILTY MIND
 may be an ingredient in crime, 222.
 evidence of, 223 *et seq.*

GUILTY POSSESSION
 may be an ingredient in crime, 228, 231.
 proof of, 229, 232.

HIGHWAY,
 procedure for obstruction of, or nuisance on, 26, 254.

HOMICIDE. *See* MANSLAUGHTER; MURDER.

HORSE,
 breach of warranty of, 51, 62.
 damage to when let on hire, 155.
 action for damage caused by unruly, 204.
 indictment for turning out vicious horse on common, 267.

HUSBAND AND WIFE. *See* MARRIED WOMAN.

ILLEGALITY
 may vitiate a contract, 62, 92.
 why evidence is admissible of, 64.
 a bond may be avoided by, 125.

IMPLIED CONTRACT,
 what it is, 48, 50.
 instances of, 49 *et seq.*, 144.
 in charter party, 75.
 when performance of work is tendered for, 79.

IMPLIED CONTRACT—*continued.*
    giving authority to master of ship, 80.
    in the case of a deed, 128, 130.
INDICTMENT,
    how to be framed in certain cases, 220.
    what it is, 221.
INDORSEMENT,
    liability on, 60.
    forged, on check, 136, 139.
INFANT,
    contract by, its nature, 45.
    presumption in favor of, when charged with felony, 248.
INNKEEPER,
    liability of to traveler, 180 *et seq.*
INSURANCE,
    cases as to policy of life, 21, 139–143.
INTENTION OF CONTRACTING PARTIES
    should, if possible, be carried out, 75, 128, 144.

JOINT STOCK COMPANY,
    contracts by promoters or directors of, 46, 48.
JUDGE,
    his duty in construing a statute, 19.
    of appellate court, his duty, 22.
JUSTICES OF THE PEACE,
    effect of conviction by them for an assault, 279.

LARCENY,
    simple, how defined, 244.
        how constituted, 244–250.
    evidence on prosecution for, 249.
    how distinguished from obtaining money, &c., by false pretenses, 263, 264, 276.
    for stealing a lamb, 270, 271.
        dead rabbits, 273.
        money from post-office savings' bank, 274.
        bank, 277.

LAW MERCHANT,
    what it is, 68.
LEGAL PRINCIPLES,
    how applied to contracts, 133 *et seq*.
        introductory remarks, 133.
        applied to the contract of suretyship, 134.
            forged check, 136.
            a life policy, 139.
    how applied to torts, 198 *et seq*.
        applied to crimes, 267 *et seq*.
            introductory remarks, 267.
            negligence in turning out vicious horse on common, 267.
            to maliciously wounding, 268.
                damaging property, 269.
                breaking window, 269.
        how applied in case of death caused by fire-works, 270.
        for stealing a lamb, 270.
LEGAL SCIENCE,
    what it concerns itself with, 17.
    necessitates use of technical terms, 35.
LENDER OF CHATTEL,
    responsibility of, 204.
LIBEL,
    malice is an ingredient in action for, 189.
    is indictable, 261.
LIFE POLICY. *See* POLICY OF LIFE INSURANCE.
LIMITATION
    of action, 118, 196.
    doctrine of, in criminal procedure, 266.
LIQUIDATED DAMAGES,
    what they are, 58.
LOST CHATTEL,
    right of finder to, 210.
LUNATIC,
    contract by, its nature, 45.
MALICE,
    in disparaging plaintiff's goods, 187.

INDEX. 303

MALICE—*continued.*
    in an action for defamation, 189.
    is often an ingredient in crime, 256 *et seq.*
    may be expressed or implied, 256, 259.
MALICIOUS PROSECUTION, 189.
MANSLAUGHTER,
    how defined, 234.
    for not supplying servant with necessaries, 253.
    for turning out vicious horse on common, 267.
    for causing death by fire-works, 267.
MARINE INSURANCE,
    good faith must be observed in, 89.
MARRIED WOMAN,
    contract by, its nature, 45.
    presumption in favor of, when charged with stealing, 247.
MASTER AND SERVANT,
    contract between, its nature, 50, 69.
    master when justified in discharging servant, 70.
    liability of master for bodily hurt to servant, 83, 84.
    damages payable to master for bodily hurt to servant, 208.
    master, when not criminally answerable for act of servant, 216, 217.
    criminal liability of master for not supplying servant with necessaries, 253.
MERCANTILE CONTRACT,
    what it is, 68.
    ingredients in, 69 *et seq.*
    how far governed by intention of parties to, 75.
    may be vitiated by fraud, 87–92.
                    illegality, 92–95.
    general remarks as to, 95.
    legal principles applied to, 134–152.
MERCANTILE USAGE,
    great weight is allowed to, 81.
    how it may operate on a contract, 81–87.
              by affixing a meaning to it, 82.
              by adding a term to it, 83.

MERCANTILE USAGE—*continued.*
    how it may operate by its inherent authority, 85.
    contracts required to be in writing, by, 42, 100.

MERGER
    of simple contract in deed, 120.

MISREPRESENTATION
    as to solvency of person, 107–109.

MONEY
    paid by mistake may be recovered, 39, 40.

MURDER,
    how defined, 234.
    evidence at trial for, 234–236.

MUTUALITY,
    nature and want of, exemplified, 75, 103.

NEGLIGENCE,
    proof of, in action against railway company, 148.
    how constituted, 169, 170.
    proof of, 170.
    contributory, 147, 171.
    action for death caused by, 173.
    liability of innkeeper for, 179 *et seq.*
    when indictable, 254, 255, 267, 270.
    by agister of a horse, 198.
    in not repairing fence, 202.
    in owner of an unruly horse, 204.
    causing death of servant, 209.

NUDUM PACTUM,
    what it is, 38.

NUISANCE,
    when indictable, 31, 254.
        actionable, 31, 166.
    may sometimes be abated or put a stop to, 33.

PARTNER,
    liability of for fraud of copartner, 91.

PATENT,
    infringement of is actionable, 156.

PENAL STATUTE
    must be construed strictly, 221.

POLICY OF LIFE INSURANCE,
    cases as to, 21, 139, 142.
    effect of fraud in regard to, 139–143.

POLICY OF MARINE INSURANCE,
    good faith must be observed in, 89.

PRESUMPTION OF LAW,
    how affected by intention of parties, 79.

PRINCIPAL AND AGENT,
    liability of principal for fraud of agent, 89, 92.

PRINCIPAL AND SURETY,
    relation between, 101–104.

PRINCIPLES
    regulate and govern our law, 23.
    are sometimes modified, 23.
    legal, applied to contracts, 133–152.
        torts, 197.
        crimes, 267 *et seq.*

PRIVITY,
    what it is, 35.
    instances of want of, 36, 40, 41, 42, 46–48.
    in a mercantile contract illustrated, 72–75.

PROMISE
    is an ingredient in a contract, 36.
    when not implied by law, 39, 40.
    is an ingredient in a mercantile contract, 72.

PROMISSORY NOTE,
    forgery of name to, its effect, 48.

PUBLIC POLICY,
    contract may be void as opposed to, 65, 127.

RAILWAY COMPANY,
    action against for loss of train, 146.
        personal hurt, 147, 148, 150.
    duty of passenger towards, 149, 151.

RATIFICATION,
    what it is, 35, 46.
    doctrine of, how applicable in a case of tort, 195.
        in criminal law, 265.

RECEIVING STOLEN GOODS,
 evidence of, 264.
REQUEST
 is an ingredient in a contract, 36.
RESCISSION OF CONTRACT,
 when allowed, 52, 54, 61, 71.
 in case of sale of goods, 77, 78, 88.
RESTRAINT OF TRADE,
 contract void as in, 65.
ROBBERY,
 how defined, 237.
 ingredients in this offense, 237.
 evidence on trial for, 238.

SALE OF GOODS,
 privity in contract respecting, 72–75.
 when performance of contract for, becomes impossible, 77.
 when contract for may be rescinded, 77, 78, 88.
 contract for, how affected by usage, 81.
 how regulated at common law, 109.
  by statute, 110 *et seq.*, 117, 118.
 by auction, 113.
 statute of limitations, how it operates in this case, 118.
SIMPLE CONTRACT. *See* CONTRACT.
 what it is, 35 *et seq*.
SIMPLE LARCENY. *See* LARCENY.
SLANDER,
 ingredients in right of action for, 189.
SOLICITOR,
 duty imposed on by his retainer, 51.
STATUTE,
 act done in evasion of, 93.
STATUTE OF FRAUDS,
 provisions of, as to guaranties, 101.
  sale of goods, 110, 113.
 effect of disregarding its provisions, 113–116.
 how extended by a more recent statute, 117.

STATUTE OF LIMITATIONS,
    its effect, 118, 119.
STATUTES,
    sometimes declare the law, 18.
    how interpreted, 19.
STATUTORY PROVISIONS
    add to the unwritten law, 18.
SURETYSHIP,
    the contract of, 75, 101 *et seq.*
            exemplified, 134–136.
TORT,
    what it is, 153.
    may consist in the invasion of a right, 153.
            instances of such a, 153–157.
    may be founded on breach of duty causing damage, 158 *et seq.*
            negligence causing damage, 169.
    may consist in a malicious act causing damage, 186–192.
            fraud causing damage, 192–194.
    instances of, 198 *et seq.*
TRESPASS
    to land, 25, 154, 251.
USAGE. *See* MERCANTILE USAGE.
VOTING CHARITIES,
    case as to, 66.
WARRANTY
    of soundness of horse, effect of breach of, 51, 62.
WRITTEN INSTRUMENTS,
    how classified, 96.
    contracts in writing, but not required to be so, 96–99.
            required to be in writing, 99–120.
            under what statutes, 100.
                a guaranty, 101.
                relation between parties to, 101–104.

THE END.

www.ingramcontent.com/pod-product-compliance
Lightning Source LLC
Chambersburg PA
CBHW021955220426
43663CB00007B/828